IT'S NOT WHERE YOU'RE GOING

IT'S HOW YOU GET THERE

Charles W. Shirriff

iUniverse, Inc.
New York   Bloomington

IT'S NOT WHERE YOU'RE GOING
IT'S HOW YOU GET THERE

Cover and photos by Kev Millikin

iUniverse books may be ordered through booksellers or by contacting:

iUniverse
1663 Liberty Drive
Bloomington, IN 47403
www.iuniverse.com
1-800-Authors (1-800-288-4677)

ISBN: 978-1-4401-1491-5 (sc)
ISBN: 978-1-4401-1490-8 (ebook)

Printed in the United States of America

iUniverse rev. date: 12/23/2008

Also by Charles W. Shirriff

Spirits of a Feather
Souls of a Feather

Dedication

To my dear wife, Wilma, for her tolerance and support.
To our amazing children, Anita and Ken (in alphabetical order),
and to their spouses, Henry and Kathryn, just for being a fantastic
part of my life.

Especially to my granddaughters, Emma, Sydney, and Lillian (left to
right) for bringing special joy and meaning into my life.

Happiness Is a Journey . . .
Not a Destination

For a long time it seemed to me that life was about to begin.

But, there was always some obstacle in the way:
something to be gotten through first,
some unfinished business,
time still to be served,
or a debt to be paid.
Then real life would begin.

At last it dawned on me that there is no way to happiness.
Happiness is the way.

So treasure every moment you have.

Work as if you don't need the money.
Love as though you have never been hurt before.
Sing like no one can hear you.
Dance as though no one is watching you.

- Father Alfred D'Souza

Contents

List of Illustrations

Acknowledgments

I wish to thank Anita, Ken, and Wilma, for their excellent advice, for providing information that I had forgotten, and for their proofreading of the manuscript.

Also, thanks to my friend, Kev Millikin, for the contribution of his picture to the cover, his inspiration for the title, his photographs, and his poem.

I also want to express my appreciation to:

- Father Alfred D'Souza for writing, '*Happiness Is a Journey . . . Not a Destination*' which so perfectly matches the title of my book and its philosophy of my life.

- A. Dowhay for having painted the picture, *Stooks*, which so beautifully illustrates to my younger readers what a 'stook' looks like.

- The Flin Flon City site for the photos of Flin Flon and of the Northern Lights on www.flinflon.net.

- The American Museum of Science, Oak Ridge, TN, for the photo graphically illustrating the effect of static electricity.

- M.C. Esher Company for permission to use a photo of one of his of amazing etchings.

I also thank the many people and organizations that have contributed information via sites on the Internet. I have tried to give specific acknowledgment whenever it was feasible for me to identify the original sources.

Prolegomenon

Don't you just hate it when an author uses a big word you've never seen before, instead of a smaller common one? I know I do. I hate having to decide whether to stop reading and look up the offending word in the dictionary—as if I can ever find one when I want to—or just ignore it and live with that nagging feeling of inadequacy. Please accept my apologies and my attempt at making it easier for you by providing the meaning of 'prolegomenon' (see * below). It really is the best word for my purposes.

In planning the structure of this book, the phrase 'dog's breakfast' comes to mind. However, I would prefer the term 'Beagle's breakfast', or maybe 'dog's dinner', because they are attractively alliterative and thus more suitable to this literary endeavor. This book is mostly a collection of short, autobiographical stories. They are not called 'chapters' because they lack the continuity of thought that such a designation implies. The sections are self-contained to make it easy for you to skip around.

The first story, 'My Love Affairs . . . With Cars' is presented as a brief overview of the events that make up the autobiographical stories that follow. This satisfies my ingrained habit of following one of the fundamental maxims of teaching: first tell them what you are going to teach, then teach it, and then tell them what you have taught.

Cars are a common thread running through most people's lives. For people like me, they become an extension of their inner self. I realize there are people who, when buying a new car, are more concerned with the number and placement of cup holders than with engine design, and for whom talk of spark plugs would put them to sleep. If you are one of those individuals you can just skip the first section and you won't have missed anything important. Everything important is revisited in later sections.

The events of my life are accurate to the best of my memory. Fortunately, I have forgotten (or chose to forget) many incidents. I have not used last names in order to provide a modicum of anonymity to individuals who were a part of the stories.

Some of the significant events in my life would require many words leading up to them when they are, in fact, self-explanatory. These vignettes are presented in italics at the end of a section to show separation from the main content. Some of these italicized items are humorous anecdotes, so feel free to laugh. You could consider them to be like Shakespearian rhyming couplets, although they are not couplets and they don't rhyme. Or, if you prefer, think of them as being like the anecdotes the Readers' Digest uses as space fillers at the end of the stories.

One other diversion is the random appearance of poetry, pictures and unrelated items between the major sections. These are to provide illumination, comic relief, a change of pace, or just because I happen to like them.

*Prolegomenon: A preliminary discussion introducing a work of considerable complexity.

"Wheat Fields"- Swift Current 1938

Introduction

By the early 1920's, the prairie grassland areas of Saskatchewan had been homesteaded into farms. The farmers soon discovered the economic value of periodically leaving each of the fields plowed but unseeded and free of weeds for a growing season. The land could rest and thus produce a better crop the next year. Unfortunately, this practice left the soil dry, powdery and susceptible to drifting, particular in years of drought. As much of the land as possible was cultivated and seeded with grain crops to maximize income. Areas of the natural prairie grass were cultivated, resulting in large unbroken stretches of fields without ground cover. Trees to act as a windbreak, or areas of grassland to catch the drifting soil, were sparse throughout the expansive areas of the prairies.

During the ten years from 1929–39, drought was widespread across the prairies of Canada and the northern United States. The dryness was broken by infrequent intervals of pounding rainstorms, which served only to create little rivers without soaking into the parched fields. Those years were called the 'The Dirty Thirties' on the prairies because of the blinding dust storms. The hot summer winds churned the topsoil into blinding clouds blowing across the fields and into the buildings. The ditches were filled with soil, and dunes were created by any obstructions such as fence posts or buildings. Attempts to seed a field were thwarted by the winds, which blew the topsoil, and the seeds, away. Sprouted crops withered in the blazing sun and from lack of rain. Farmers began moving into the towns and cities in search of work and a pay cheque.

In a cruel coincidence of fate, this was also the time of the major stock market crash leading to a nationwide depression. City people who lost their money in the stock market crash sought to find a less money-oriented life in rural areas. They hoped to find work, or at least sustenance, on a small farm. At the same time when farmers were leaving the farms in search of non-existent jobs in the cities, penniless

1

city folk were trying to move into the rural areas. No one escaped unaffected by the 'perfect storm' created by the Great Depression and the Dirty Thirties.

I was born in Saskatchewan during the Dirty Thirties. I missed the early part of the Dirty Thirties experience by not being born until 1933 (the year when the recession hit its lowest point, ushering in the Great Depression). Then I slept through the next few years of it.

The Roaring Twenties would have been a much better time in which to have been born, but somehow I don't recall having a choice at the time. Or, if the New Age people really are right in their belief that pre-born babies get to choose their place and circumstances of birth, I must have just chosen poorly.

CANADIAN CITIES/TOWNS IN WHICH I LIVED UP TO AGE TWENTY-FIVE

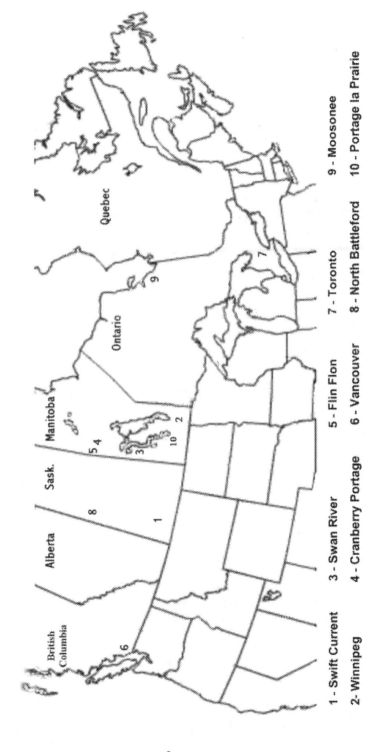

1 - Swift Current

2- Winnipeg

3 - Swan River

4 - Cranberry Portage

5 - Flin Flon

6 - Vancouver

7 - Toronto

8 - North Battleford

9 - Moosonee

10 - Portage la Prairie

My Love Affairs . . . With Cars

My love affair with cars started in November of 1940 when I was about 7 years old (give or take a year or two). It began with an Eaton's Mail Order Catalogue, which listed a pedal-driven car in just my size. I studied the picture of that car and memorized every detail. I know it was November because I decided, as only a person that age can decide, that I was going to get that pedal car as a Christmas present. I even knew it would be my Aunt Isabel who was going to give it to me, without having had any conversations with her about it. She lived in Vancouver and operated a small antique shop, so in my mind she must have had lots of spare money. I really don't know why I thought all that. I just did.

It didn't matter that we had several early snowfalls that year. After every snowstorm, I would go outside and shovel a 'race track' in the snow, complete with curves and loops, carefully cleaned to ground level to make the pedaling at least possible, if not easy. Even at such an early age, I was concerned only with the journey and not with any identifiable goal.

I didn't get that car for Christmas. In fact, I never did get to see it 'in the flesh' so to speak. Thus my unrequited first love affair with a car was astonishingly short and quickly forgotten.

My older brother, my parents and I lived on a small farm about fifteen minute's drive from the city of Swift Current, in the province of Saskatchewan. Transportation was a major part of our life. Obviously, we needed at least one car and a truck for hauling grain. I recall at least twice when we had a small private airplane fly out from town and land on a nearby field to take my father to town to buy groceries because of snow-blocked roads.

When I was in Grade 11, I had a driver's license. Farm boys in those days could get a license at age fourteen to help in hauling grain to the elevators. On special occasions, I would have the use my father's newish (he never drove a car more than 4 years old) 1949 hydromatic Chevrolet to drive to the city. It was a nice car and it would happily do 70 mph (110 km/hr) on our gravel highways, as long as one was careful to avoid the loose gravel ridges.

Somewhere, probably from an advertising brochure at the dealership, I had learned that the hydromatic automatic transmission was relatively indestructible because it was a fluid connection. They said it wouldn't hurt the transmission if one were to shift from drive into reverse while the car was moving. They were right. Even at high speeds the back wheels would spin furiously in reverse and bring the car to a shuddering stop, provided the engine was revved up enough to avoid stalling. It was an interesting alternative to using the brakes, and it didn't ruin the transmission, at least not before it was traded in on a new car. The Chevy was a good 'transportation' car, but not a car with which I developed any emotional relationship, or even any degree of respect (obviously).

I did learn the magical feeling of privacy, security and safety when one is alone at night in a car, or with another person in it. It was like being in my own private world.

I started my first real relationship with a car that same year. It was a 1929 Model A Ford. It wasn't really mine, but my mother and I had pretty much exclusive use of it, and I could do all sorts of improper things to it.

For instance, we just happened to have a wartime surplus airplane in our yard. The airplane had been disabled so the engine would not run (in spite of my best efforts), but it had an endless supply of switches, hydraulic pumps and other interesting things. We also had a war surplus truck (with right-hand drive), a 4-wheel-drive jeep, and a few other things like a flamethrower, all in good working order. It may sound strange now, but at that time many people acquired them for very little money. I installed a pair of airplane headlights on the car and had them work with auxiliary fuses and switches also from the airplane. They provided excellent lighting on dark roads—and a frequently dead battery.

SOME OF MY FAVORITE CARS

1931 Ford Model A Coupe

1971 Karmann Ghia

Mercedes-Benz 300SL Gull-wing

Morris Minor circa 1941

It was a marvelous car. Whenever my mother drove it alone we could count on a story.

"I don't know why, but the motor stopped running half way to town," my mother said.

"You mean it wouldn't start?" I asked.

"It wouldn't do anything. I thought it was ruined."

"So what did you do?"

"This nice man stopped and said it was out of water. He went to a farm and got some water for it."

"And it runs now?"

"As far as I know."

I checked the car. It was fine. It had run out of water, overheated, and the engine had seized up. All it needed was a drink of water to cool it down. A car with a newer, tighter engine would have been ruined.

Another time my mother and I were driving along the highway toward Swift Current.

"That's strange. What is that over there in the field?" she asked.

I looked into the field and noticed a wheel rolling merrily across the ditch and through the field.

"I don't know. Maybe you should stop."

She pulled off to the side of the road. We got out and looked around at the car, neither of us knowing what we were looking for.

I looked where the left rear wheel should have been. As the old Irish saying goes, 'there it was—gone'. The wheel in the field belonged to us. I chased after it until I caught it and brought it back to the car. I took one of the lug nuts off each of the other three wheels to attach the errant one, and we were on our way. No damage was done.

In winter, if the car didn't want to start at minus 35 degrees all that was needed was a kettle of hot water poured over the intake manifold, and maybe a quarter-cup of gasoline down the carburetor. If it had been sitting in the cold so long that the oil was thick and the motor would not turn over, a bit of gasoline ignited in a pan and pushed under the engine heated the car's oil pan with no damage. How could anyone help falling in love with a car like that? Just don't try putting a small fire under a modern computer-dependent car with electrical wiring everywhere.

After I graduated from high school, I went to the University of Manitoba as a car-less freshman. I was living in residence and city bus service was adequate, but I missed having a car.

The summer after 1st year, my father bought me an old 1939 Chevy. That was very kind of him, but he and his friendly neighborhood used car salesman had no idea what I really wanted in a car. I spent my spare time that summer replacing the head gasket with a thinner one designed to increase the compression ratio. This would increase the horsepower to what I considered a respectable amount. I hoped this would increase its original mediocre performance to a level that would allow me to accept it as at least a potential object of my affection. The transformation was successful and resulted in an amazing exhaust sound, rather like a high-pitched miniature wind tunnel on steroids.

My university roommate, Len, met me in Swift Current and we headed back on the 12-hour drive to the university. Unfortunately, the car was not up to the task and threw a main bearing two hours short of our destination. It wasn't the car's fault. I had requested that the main bearings be replaced (re-babbitted, to be precise) but, as I found out later, the garage had made a decision that the old bearings should be fine because those cars had a low compression engine. It was my oversight in not telling them that it was actually becoming a high compression engine.

We limped to the nearest town and traded the Chevy for a 1950 Frazer (of Kaiser-Frazer fame). It was love at first sight. The car was old, luxurious, cheap and unusual—the perfect match for me. Its 'free wheeling' feature won it a special place in my heart. There was a lever one could pull out when driving on the highway and it would allow the engine to idle while the car coasted silently along at highway speed. Technically speaking, the engine could drive the wheels when you wanted to speed up, but the wheels would not slow the engine down as a braking action, as in most cars. Pushing in the lever reconnected the wheels to the engine. Now, this might not seem to be very useful, which is probably why so few cars, before or since, ever had that feature. The attraction for me was the total silence as the car coasted along at highway speed with the engine idling. It was somewhat the same psychological effect as that of a turbocharged engine in a modern car—the car can accelerate without increasing engine noise. OK, so it isn't exactly the same, but that is the closest thing to it I have experienced.

The Frazer and I parted company later that year after my roommate plowed it into the back of a city bus. It wasn't his fault. I would have done the same thing. The bus route was through an unpopulated area on the way to the university and I'd never seen it stop at that bus stop. Obviously, sometimes it did. I collected the insurance but didn't buy another car for four years. It may not have been a coincidence that I had been keeping track of expenses and had discovered that it was costing me more to keep my car running than it did to provide myself with food and lodging. The conclusion was inescapable. I have never kept track of car expenses again since then, except for income tax purposes.

Fast-forward through four car-deprived years. I had graduated with a B. Sc., and had taught for one year at the Swan River High School in northern Manitoba, intending just to make enough money to go back to university for my master's degree in science.

However, I enjoyed teaching so much I decided to get my degree in education. One of my students, Al, had a married sister in Vancouver and he planned to attend university there in the fall. He and two of his friends, Jack and Mel, decided to go there with him. I have no idea why I went with them. It just seemed like right thing to do at the time.

The four of us went to Vancouver in July after the school year ended. The university was across the city from where we would be living. Obviously, it would be most efficient to have a small, old, cheap car instead of paying four bus fares every day. We visited a used car lot. None of us had ever seen or heard of the British made Morris Minor, but the salesman said it would be perfect for us because it got fantastically good gas mileage and it was cheap.

It was a dinky little car, rather more like the pedal car I had wanted as a child than a real car. It had a 'bullet proof' motor, as the car magazines liked to say. It never failed to start immediately and to run smoothly, even the one time when I discovered a hole the size of a quarter in the top one of its four tiny pistons. Another time, on a trip to Flin Flon with my friend, Jack, the car stopped running as if it were out of gas. I discovered the electric fuel pump was not pumping. We drove the last hour with the hood open and Jack draped over one fender so he could flick the fuel pump contact every 10 seconds. It did slow us down a little because I didn't want to see him flying off the fender and into the ditch at highway speed.

There was another time when I was getting ready to go from Flin Flon to Vancouver. I discovered one of my tires had worn through the rubber so that the bare cords were showing. I had no spare and certainly no one in northern Manitoba sold tiny tires in the size needed. There seemed to be no choice but to drive to Winnipeg and get a new tire there. No one in Winnipeg carried that foreign size tire, so I just kept driving hoping I could make it to Brandon . . . and then Regina . . . then Calgary . . . and eventually Vancouver. I had traveled some 40 hours on a threadbare tire—lucky for me it was such a light car. I did finally get a new tire in Vancouver. Some people might say I should have purchased a spare tire at the same time, but obviously, I really didn't need one. So, I didn't buy a spare tire.

The salesman was right about the gasoline mileage. We didn't care much about mileage when we bought it because at that time gasoline was only 25 cents per gallon. However, I was glad for it one time when I was driving back to Manitoba via the United States through the International Peace Gardens Park late at night in the off-season. I was almost out of gas and all the gas stations were closed, with the pumps turned off. Desperation is the mother of invention (to misquote Victor Hugo and many others). I think that car must have come with its own built-in guardian angel to lead me to those gas pumps.

I tried draining the gas from the hose at a gas pump. To my delight I found I could straighten out the hose and drain about half a cup of gas, caught in the loop of the hose, into my tank. So I went from pump to pump pulling the hoses straight and draining them. I drove for two hours by stopping at every gas station and draining the hoses until I found a station that was open. With the price of gas as it is now I may have to resort to draining the hoses at closed gas stations again.

Besides, it was a green convertible. The British were very fond of British green for their Morris Minors. I have never seen one in any other color except in pictures. I had never had a convertible and I assumed it would be awesome in Vancouver in the summer. Of course, I had no idea how much it rained in Vancouver in the summer time, but I loved it on the beautiful sunny days they also have.

That car served us for the year and then took Jack and me to the mining town of Flin Flon for summer employment. We both worked underground initially and made pretty good money. In the fall we returned to Vancouver with the intention of continuing our studies there.

A lot can happen in a summer. Al and his girlfriend suddenly realized they needed to get married—and soon. Her parents were not thrilled, to say the least, and strongly forbade the marriage. Al asked if they could borrow my car to elope. It was such a romantically exciting idea I couldn't resist signing the car over to him, for the nominal fee of one dollar, as a wedding present. They sped across the U.S. border heading for Winnipeg as fast as the tiny, 10-year-old, 30-horsepower, Morris Minor would take them. Her parents discovered their plan in the morning and took off after them in their new V-8 Chrysler. The chase was on.

Their 10-hour head start was enough. By the time the parents arrived in Winnipeg, Al and his new bride had left the church. A few months later, I was named godfather of their first child. Years later, I was invited to their 25th wedding anniversary.

Maybe it was Al's example of how to grab hold of life and make it work for you. Or maybe I just realized I was coming back to more of what I had left in May. Whatever it was, I decided that if the Faculty of Education represented what teaching was all about then I wasn't interested in pursuing it. I happened upon an ad for a Meteorology course at the University of Toronto starting in January. I applied for the program and, without waiting to be accepted, bought an old car to drive to Toronto. At that time I just assumed I would get any job for which I applied. It may have been that I didn't apply for many jobs, or I was just lucky.

It was an old 2-door Plymouth—strictly a transportation car. I was accustomed to driving the Morris Minor at full throttle on the highway and drove the Plymouth the same way. It got most of the way to Toronto before the engine blew up in clouds of steam and hot oil. I didn't have time to become attached to it, which was just as well because I don't think we were really compatible. I didn't even consider it as a friend.

I arrived in Toronto, by Greyhound, with my metal suitcase containing all my worldly belongings. The professors at the university kindly gave me work in the Meteorological department organizing research data and general office work until my course began in January. One of my early tasks was processing application forms. I was surprised to find myself looking at my own application form. It was an easy one to do. I didn't need to check my references, and I approved it with dispatch.

Life was good. I had a job and a future as a meteorologist. I thought I knew where I was going and how to get there. All I needed was a car. Toronto was full of used car lots. I spent many happy hours car shopping. The 1957 gull-wing Mercedes sports car was fantasy-love at first sight, but clearly out of my league in every imaginable way. It was like falling in love with a movie star—gorgeous but unattainable.

An old square-fender MG-TC was tempting too, but a bit pricey for its age and performance, and somehow didn't seem to fit my self-image. So I fell back on my first true love—another Morris Minor in British green and a convertible. It was as if my previous car and I had been reunited to begin my new life.

A year and a half later, near the end of August, the world was getting ready for the beginning of a new school year. I became restless as I recalled how much I had enjoyed my year of teaching in Swan River. I sold my beloved Morris Minor for a dollar—rapidly becoming my standard selling price to friends—to my roommate at the time, and took a bus back to Winnipeg.

And so ended my fickle love affairs with a variety of old cars. My plan, if one can call it a plan, was to either return to teaching or to go to Mexico where my saved money would be adequate for me to live on the beach for at least a year. It was too difficult a decision for me to think about so I flipped a coin. I don't remember if I won or lost the toss, but the coin sent me back to teaching. I had learned how to make a coin flip work for me. I would make my call; heads Mexico, tails teaching. If it had come up for Mexico and I felt disappointed, I had my answer . . . teaching. If it had come up teaching and I felt good, then that was my answer. The coin served only to focus my feelings.

It was late in the summer and there were only a few schools with an opening on their teaching staff. I chose Cranberry Portage, which was a tiny community in northern Manitoba, between Swan River and Flin Flon. It was a familiar area (you have to drive through it to get to Flin Flon) and I was dissatisfied with life in big cities. A small isolated rural setting might help me get my life together.

While teaching at Cranberry Portage, I chose my first-ever NEW car by reading magazines and looking at brochures. It was to be a 1959 Triumph TR3A. They were not at all common in Canada and available only in Toronto. So I bought a one-way ticket on Air Canada and flew back to Toronto to meet the car I had only seen in pictures. Little did I suspect that I would be sharing the rest of my life with this unknown car.

With a minimum down payment and three years of payments it was all mine. It was a British racing car, and as such, should have been in British racing green. However, in my mind, green was the color reserved for Morris Minors. I wanted it red. But the red ones came with red interiors and I had found red interiors to be emotionally upsetting for me. So I bought a white one with black upholstery. Within two years it was repainted and the way I wanted it—red with black upholstery.

It had a four-speed manual transmission, with overdrive on the top three gears, giving it seven forward speeds. I learned to drive it on the trip back to Manitoba and fortunately I was very impressed with it. It had never occurred to me that I might find the car to be totally unsuitable for city or highway driving, and I had made no plans for that possibility. I just knew I wanted it from what brochures and car magazines had told me.

When I read in the manual that the car should be driven at no more than 3500 rpm for the first 500 miles, I was taken aback, thinking I was going to have a slow first 500 miles on my drive home. My fears were unfounded. When I first took the car out onto the highway, I discovered that in 4th gear overdrive, at 3500 rpm, I was traveling 78 mph (120 km/hr. That was more than the speed limit and thus I felt it was at least adequate for the trip home.

First gear is generally not used for starting up (unless you want to lay two tracks of rubber or are starting uphill on a mountain slope).

Around the city, second and third gears were more than enough, especially considering that there is the option of overdrive on both.

There were (at least) two downsides to the car. One was that it hated idling. It would overheat anytime it was kept to a slow pace such as in city traffic situations. The other was that it was very difficult to find a garage that wanted to do even the simplest work on it. I found it easier to do maintenance work on it myself. I should have clued in that having only one dealership in all of Canada did not bode well for servicing opportunities. But then, I have never said I was smart—good in school, yes—but not necessarily smart. I soon discovered that I couldn't even leave it in a garage for a tire change without returning to be met by an irate mechanic demanding, "Get this %@#* car out of here."

It wasn't that they hated the car; they just didn't know how to release the parking brake to get it out of the garage. You see, it's a racing car. The 'parking brake' was designed to be used as a 'racing' brake. It works only on the back wheels and is used when the driver wants to control a skid. Hence, it is designed so that that pulling the lever did not make it catch and hold, as do 'normal' cars, unless you held down the button. When the mechanic automatically pushed the button (expecting to release the brake) and gave it a tug, the brake would just hold more tightly. Repeating this action several times ended up with the back wheels becoming more and more firmly locked. When I would arrive, pull the lever (without holding the button down) and release the brake, it somehow didn't improve their temper. I tried having a sign on the dash saying, 'DO NOT HOLD THE PARKING BRAKE BUTTON DOWN'. Unfortunately, they would either not see it, or if they did, it didn't make sense to them so they would ignore it. The only effective solution was to stay at the garage with my car while it was there.

It was the fastest accelerating thing on the road in its time, and still might be except for its progressively more common old age problems.

That was some 50 years ago and I still have my original Triumph. Although we don't play together as much anymore we have a standing date to go out together for parades. I get it in shape for the event and it finds new ways to develop last-minute ailments.

I've had flings of convenience with other cars, some good and some not so much, over the years and probably will continue to do so. We went on a road trip with our children, ages 8 and 11, to Ontario in a nice new Volvo station wagon. We bought it because it was highly rated for safety, even though it was ugly and stodgy. On our visit to the Canadian National Exhibition, we parked in the 'Go Train' parking lot near Lake Ontario and took the train to the exhibition grounds. After spending an enjoyable afternoon of rides and displays, we took the train back to the parking lot.

There had been some rain during the afternoon, and it seemed to look progressively wetter the closer we got to the parking lot. When we arrived, it became evident that a waterspout had passed over the area and had flooded the parking lot. The water was about two feet deep around our car. It had soaked our sleeping bags, luggage, and ruined our 8 mm movie camera. We got things dried out as best we could with the help of our friend's wet and dry shop vacuum. My first surprise came when I pulled the shoulder belt across my chest to buckle up. It was soaking wet from the water trapped in its holder and sloshed as it slapped water across my chest. It was even more amusing when we turned on our windshield wipers and discovered that the radio turned on and off with them. When we got home I traded in the car for one without the automatic radio feature.

I must mention the 1971 Karmann Ghia I bought in 1989 for my daughter, Anita, to drive when she went to high school in Winnipeg. I could have fallen in love with it because it had a beautiful body design. But it was built with the Volkswagen Beetle chassis and engine. Not that I have had anything against the Beetle, and I admire the engineering of its engine, but it was somehow not being honest. It looked like a high power sports car. I've had people at gas stations ask if it were a Porsche, but its performance was that of a Beetle. It struck me as somehow deceitful to be so beautiful without comparable performance. I sold it when Anita didn't need it anymore . . . but it wasn't easy because she was so beautiful. (I meant the car, not Anita . . . although Anita is beautiful, too).

One of my fun times with a car was traveling with my wife, Wilma, in Germany on the Autobahn. It had either had no speed limit, or a speed limit based on the car's engine size. The bigger your engine, the higher the speed limit was for you. We were in a rented Ford Fiesta replete with a tiny 4-cylinder engine. It was a game little car that would respond to my flooring the gas pedal with a loud roar from the motor as it shifted down, but no noticeable increase in speed. However, it didn't object to traveling all day at its top speed of 70 mph (110 km/hr). We had the experience of seeing Porsches appear in the rearview mirror, whip past us as if we were standing still and then disappear over the horizon in a flash. I thought someday I would like to go back to Germany and cruise the Autobahn in a rented Porsche. However, seeing the cost of Porsche rentals (and some of the accident scenes on the Autobahn) made me decide I should wait until I had a terminal ailment so I wouldn't be risking too many good years of my life. Imagine my chagrin when I discovered rental companies don't rent Porsches to old people. I wonder why.

Wilma and I made two trips to Europe with our children, Anita and Ken, and traveled in rented cars. I discovered that the different racial stereotypes were clearly reflected in their driving habits. In Spain the people tended to be aggressive in their attitude and speech. This was reflected in their driving. It was as if they were seemingly acting out a bullfight. Although the roads had beautifully smooth, paved shoulders, the drivers would never use them, not even to avoid the oncoming traffic when one car was passing another. You could almost hear the cries of '¡Ole!' as the car pulled back into its lane at the last possible moment. Maybe they would use the paved shoulder if it were absolutely essential to avoid a collision, but fortunately, I never had the opportunity to experience this.

Crossing the border from Spain into Portugal presented a totally different type of driver. The Portuguese are a polite, mild-mannered and gentle people. This was reflected in their highway driving and in their way of life. One time I was driving the wrong way for a few yards down a back street to get to our parking place. A man who saw us coming pointed his finger toward the ground and waved it, and his head, gently from side-to-side. In Spain we would have heard about it in emphatic Spanish and perhaps a more pointed hand gesture.

The British, of course, very properly drove on the wrong side of the road as if it that were the only possibility and obeyed the rules of the road politely and formally. Only the British could consider a roundabout to be a logical method of turning a corner. In fairness to them, I must admit roundabouts are surprisingly efficient and avoid the left turn accidents common in North American. It takes a while to get used to the idea of suddenly having cars on both sides of you driving at different speeds in a circle. At least they are all going the same direction.

The emotional and spontaneous Italians were an experience. When stopping for a red light they would move over and line up to fill all the lanes, resulting in two sold lines of traffic, half of them on the wrong side of the road, facing each other. When the light changed green both sides drove forward at full speed, gradually merging and dodging their way to the proper side of the road. Fortunately, their cars tended to be small and nimble. It was efficient but very surprising the first time I unexpectedly found myself in the middle of it.

Germans drove with precision and determination. Instructions to other drivers (such as blinking their headlights to signal they were going to pass you) were clear and consistent, with the expectation that you would know what they meant and would do as you were told (as in, get out of the way of my speeding Porsche).

I think my love affairs with cars are now over. I must admit I did arrange to have a look at a new Ferrari in a showroom in California recently—very nice, but not really my type. I'm afraid she might be too much for me. Maybe if I were 50 years younger?

Besides, I have the Triumph parked in my garage.

***

~ Communication Problems ~

Driving my new Triumph home from Toronto for the first time, I stopped at a small city gas station for a quart of oil. The manual specified Castrol motor oil (a very common brand of British motor oil).

I asked the station attendant: "Do you have 'Castrol oil?'"

The service person replied seriously: "You'll have to go to a drug store for that."

Maybe my Canadian accent confused him.

***

~ An Old Family Story ~
(from Life in Porcupine Plain, Saskatchewan)

Annie returns to the house after picking berries in the bush and says: "I heard a bear out there in the bush."

Jess: "So what did you do?"

Annie: "Well, I said loudly, 'My, isn't it a hot day, Jess?'"

Jess: "Why did you say, 'Jess' when you were alone?"

Annie: " Well, I didn't want the bear to think I was by myself."

~ Photo ~

by Kev Millikin

upon the dust lined shelf
amongst my most valued possessions
there stands a photo of my most recent obsession
the highest incredible being
inside and out
has crossed my path to lead me in what life is about
to see, to hear, to taste it all
is nothing
if you do not feel and allow yourself to fall
to trust in his faith
and to be one in our eyes
this bond is so intimate
we must never say good-bye.
Though you are not here beside me
I press my finger to your photo
you are here with me
this I do know
I feel your presence, warm inside
I know you are thinking of me
you are my star guide.
As pinholes in a blanket
the light shines through
there is this amazing force
that enwraps me and you
from the tips of heaven
to the depths of hell
you are my angel. . .
and with you
only time will tell.

"FISHING" ON THE FARM AT SWIFT CURRENT
Bill & Clifford - 1937

The Early Years

It is a fact that I was born on September 17th, 1933, in Regina, capital city of the province of Saskatchewan. I think I have been told it was at 2:35 AM, but I don't know for sure. It seems like a reasonable time to me. I don't recall ever being told why I was born in Regina when my mother (Letitia Anne), father (Clifford NMI), and 2½ year older brother (also Clifford NMI), lived on a smallish farm, near the city of Swift Current (population of 5000 at that time), a 3-hour drive west of Regina. I was christened Charles William but was always called Bill, for reasons I was never told nor understood. This eventually resulted in my being randomly called Bill, Billy, William, Willie, Charles, Charlie, and even Chuck, at various times as an adult.

I've often wondered why my brother and father got only one name between them (with **No Middle Initial**) while I got at least two all just for me. I have long suspected this was the beginning of my tendency to embrace multiple personalities to match my various names (or moods).

Our family survived the Dirty 30's better than many people, partly because my father worked for periods of time at the Swift Current Experimental Station. During the Dirty Thirties, he helped establish remedial farming practices such as alternating crop fields with areas of grass or alfalfa (strip-farming) and planting fast-growing tree belts to break the force of the winds. The face of Saskatchewan slowly changed from being just bare flat prairie, to become flat prairie with clumps of trees and strips of grass or hay. Dugouts became common on many farms as a way of collecting and holding water to get the livestock though the hot dry summers.

The 'fishing' picture was taken on our farm, probably to show what could be done on the dry prairie. It was obviously a posed picture—my brother and I weren't gullible enough to think there would be fish in an artificial dugout that often dried up by the end of summer. Or maybe it had been stocked with some kind of experimental fish, for all I know. I really don't remember.

His job provided some income, but I do recall hearing a lot about 'the starving Armenians' when I didn't want to eat my vegetables, so I assume they were worse off than we were. I didn't quite understand how my eating vegetables would help them in any significant way unless it was their vegetables I was or wasn't eating. In that case, wouldn't they be better off if I didn't eat them so maybe they could? I didn't invest very much time trying to resolve this problem.

My father also periodically announced, "It's time for an austerity program."

I did understand that this meant we were spending no money for anything until further notice. That I could understand.

His work had side benefits; such as our house having a 12-volt battery operated electrical lighting system (and later a 120-volt generator that would start when you tried to turn on a light) at a time long before the rural areas began being serviced by commercial hydroelectric power. The Experimental Station needed to run trials of new technologies and equipment and we were convenient and willing guinea pigs. There were probably a lot of other experimental goodies of which I was not aware. I do remember we got a special, secret rhubarb root, which was not commercially available. I didn't notice any difference, but everyone else raved about how red and sweet it was.

One other source of income for the family was my father's work with a horse marketing board to sell horsemeat overseas, primarily to Belgium where it was a delicacy. At the time of the depression, the Prairies had a lot of horses made surplus by the change from horse drawn implements to tractors for fieldwork. The grasslands had suffered from the drought and the constantly drifting soil, leaving little to feed the horses. The sale of horsemeat from Canada, which began out of necessity in the 1930's to reduce a surplus of horses, has continued to the present time. Live horses are shipped to Canada and Mexico from the United States for 'processing' and the meat shipped back to the United States.

Our house was a large, two-story, stone building. The area under the house had been excavated to provide space for a coal burning furnace, a large coal storage area, a root cellar, and a couple of rustic storage rooms. The walls and floors were roughly hewn dirt and there was no provision for light or ventilation. For some reason, this dark, damp, stale area didn't terrify me as much as it should have, maybe because I didn't have to feed coal to the furnace. The heated water circulated on the principle of convection, more or less, to radiators throughout the house. The expansion tank upstairs in my bedroom, would overflow a few times every winter.

The cultivated land around the homestead was sandy and not very fertile for growing grain crops. A good wheat crop would yield maybe 15 bushels per acre, compared with a Manitoba crop of 40 bushels per acre. The low yield was somewhat offset by the lower cultivating costs. Even the weeds didn't grow well. We also grew wheat, some barley, oats and alfalfa for feed. Most of the straw was baled for animal bedding in the winter.

Harvest in those days consisted of cutting crops with a binder that tied them with a length of 'binder twine' into bundles called sheaves (as in the hymn, 'bringing in the sheaves'). They would then be butted onto the ground and tipped toward each other at the top to form miniature tipis of 4, 6 or more sheaves to make a 'stook'. It would be an even number because a person would grab one sheaf in each hand by the twine. They would dry in the field before being fed into a threshing machine or forked onto a wagon to be taken to the barn to be stored as feed for the livestock. Both the process of stooking and the tossing of sheaves into a wagon with a pitchfork was better upper body exercise than any modern gym equipment. My bulging biceps in Grades 6–8 were the envy of my classmates at a time when comparing the development of body parts was an important activity. I wasn't nearly as successful in other body-part competitions. Don't ask.

We also raised a constantly changing variety of animals of different kinds and breeds. They provided a multitude of experiences and I learned a wide assortment of skills, only some of which proved useful later in life.

Milking the cows was one such limited-use experience. The cows would come to the barn when I called them (they knew there would be food in the manger) and would go directly into their own stall. When they put their heads through the stanchion in order to get their hay, the stanchion would be closed to hold their head secure. The rest of the cow was free to move around—a disturbing experience when you are seated right against her stomach, close to her right-rear leg, and within swatting range of her often wet and usually dirty tail.

Some cows would stand patiently while they were being milked. Others would try to kick the milk pail away and required the use of anti-kick 'leg cuffs' which loosely constrained their back legs to each other. The assumption was that when the cow tried to kick with one leg the other leg would restrain it. This usually worked well . . . except for the times when the restraining leg would be pulled out from under the cow and I would end up with a cow sitting on my lap while I tried to hold the partially filled pail of milk safely out of the way with one hand and the cow with the other.

Another useful tactic was to have the cow's tail clamped by a gopher trap tied to the back wall. Even with the best of planning, one would never get through a week of twice-a-day milking without at least once having a cow put its foot into the half-full milk pail or kicking it (and me) over.

The best part of milking was feeding a barn cat fresh warm milk directly from the teat. The cat would sit well back behind the cow (out of range of a kick) and wait expectantly for me to shoot a stream of really fresh, warm milk close to him. The cat would adjust its position and lick the milk right out of the air as it was shot close to him. It could drink stream after stream without missing a drop—its little pink tongue just a continuous blur.

We also raised sheep of assorted breeds, probably as research for the Experimental Station. I can't think of any other reason for having continually changing breeds, especially when sheep were not a common farm animal in our area. Sheep were a good preparation for a lot of things. They taught me how hard it is to herd them, not unlike a lot of people I was to meet in my later life. They would follow a lead sheep without any concern about what sheep that happened to be at the time; but they would not be herded. They would run off to the side, or back from where they came. They would do anything but go where they were supposed to go.

STOOKS

Bill and Cliff stooking

Painting by A. Dowhay

Enter Jim—40 pounds of black and white Border Collie sheep dog. He was trained to respond to whistle, voice and hand motions to herd livestock of any size and in any number with amazing skill and enthusiasm. On command, he could separate one or more specific sheep from a flock using one-on-one nipping and pushing.

Occasionally, a sheep might challenge his authority and they would have a stare down. Jim always won, with the sheep turning tail and going where directed. The same thing would happen with a full-grown bull. Jim would win, often easily dodging a well-aimed kick as the bull turned and ran away. He would herd any animal from a cat to a horse. He was an incorrigible car chaser, running close beside the tire and nipping at it. He knew no fear. Anything that moved seemed to trigger his built-in motion detector and innate love of herding. I have met a number of people with these same characteristics, but they never had the same degree of finesse as was exhibited by Jim.

I did find the experience of shearing a sheep, which weighed as much as I did, to be satisfying as well as challenging. The sheep did not share my enthusiasm, but most of them were relaxed and accepting of the process unless the shears accidentally nicked them. I never did well with hand shears, but power shears were almost fun. After being shorn of their wool, the sheep would be run through a trough of sheep dip to kill the ubiquitous sheep ticks, which are like wood ticks but with a more aggressive attitude. The smell of sheep dip, and the oily feel of the wool, not to mention having to check for tics before going to bed, made it less fun than you might expect.

We also raised goats for several years. And yes, they really do enjoy sneaking up behind you and butting you severely . . . and repeatedly. I've tried drinking goat's milk, and I accept that it is very good for you, but the look of the glass with its thick, lumpy white coating after you empty it was more than I could handle emotionally.

The cultivated part of our farm was smallish, but was augmented by a large area of pastureland rented on a 99-year lease from the municipality. It was mostly hilly and rocky with a large ravine (good for a short downhill ski in the winter), but it did have a small spring trickling into a pond, making it ideal for grazing livestock.

We had a few horses. I spent many happy hours riding 'my' horse (named Charlie) around the pasture fixing the fences and checking on the whereabouts and welfare of the cattle. I think he was designated as being mine because he was big, headstrong, and restless. He loved galloping and jumping over ditches. He casually bucked me off more times than I could count. I'm sure he didn't think of it as bucking and would think, "Dumb kid. He fell off, again."

He and I were kindred spirits, although I kept my restless spirit better hidden than he did. The rest of the family wasn't as keen on adventurous riding expeditions and preferred horses with more agreeable temperaments.

We were a fifteen-minute drive from the nearest schools in Swift Current. Usually my brother and I took a school bus that turned off the highway and then traveled a mile and a half along a dirt road to pick us up at our door. However, it didn't take much rain or snow to discourage the bus driver, resulting in our missing quite a bit of school time. Sometimes in the winter, we would have to take a shortcut across the snow-covered field on skis until the roads were cleared through the snowdrifts. Usually, I would have to pull my bulky euphonium (you'll hear more than you want to know about the euphonium in the next section) on a toboggan. When the snowfall was particularly heavy, the rural municipality would run a snowplow down the road to push the snow off into the ditches. Sometimes we would stay in town overnight in inclement weather. When my own children were young I'm sure they got tired of my stories beginning with, "You think that's bad? When I was your age . . ."

There were periods of time when we stayed in town with relatives. Aunt Isabel's father lived in town several blocks from the school and she sometimes lived there. The walk from her place to school included what seemed to me to be a huge hill with the school at the top. Actually, a lot of my memories of Swift Current involve walking up hills. My junior high school was at the top of a different hill. I have very few memories of ever walking down hills.

Maybe the prairies aren't really as flat as everyone says. Maybe they are more like a part of the artist Escher's world with endless stairs going on forever.

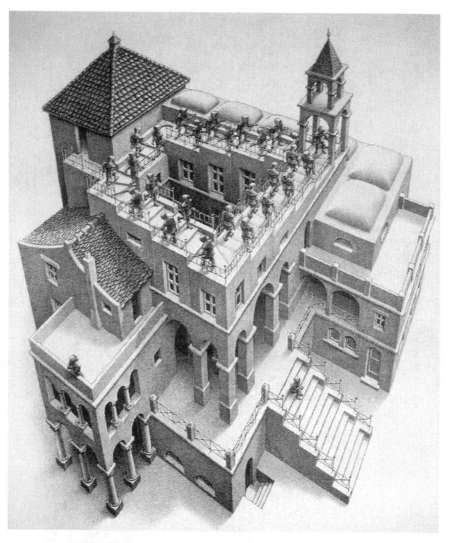

M.C. Escher's "Ascending and Descending"
(c) 2008 The M.C. Escher Company - the Netherlands.
All rights reserved. Used by permission. www.mcescher.com

One day when I was in primary school, maybe Grade 2, I confused the recess bell with the dismissal bell and walked to Aunt Isabel's place, as was my custom, and played outside in the back yard. I remember having an absolutely lovely time playing in some mud and making paths in it—probably for the non-existent pedal car in my imagination. I did think a few times that someone should be picking me up to take me home soon, but the thought quickly passed. Eventually I was picked up to go back to the farm. I had enjoyed a long, quiet time playing. I do vaguely remembered being in trouble for being messy with mud and for having worried everyone by disappearing for over an hour. Mostly I remember it as a lovely afternoon. If I'd had the chance I would have happily done it again.

In Grade 6, I decided I needed to have some claim to fame. Scholastically, I was always at the top of my class, but it wasn't satisfying to me because there was no challenge in achieving success. I got high marks with no work because, or so I thought, my classmates were not the brightest kids on the block. My first major search for a *raison d'etre* resulted in my becoming entranced with magic. I discovered a company that would send me their free catalog listing literally hundreds of magic tricks and equipment with prices ranging from a few cents to a few hundred dollars each. The catalogue was at least 3 inches thick and provided me with hours of engrossed study. Although the secrets of the tricks were not revealed in the catalog, many of them had enough description for me to discern their processes. The ones I purchased (courtesy of my parents' generosity) included detailed lines of patter to go with the presentation, making it easy for me to become more of a showman than my congenital nature would have predicated. I learned to be an actor. I also learned a lot of other things through my adventures with magic, not the least of which was not to be gullible. Years later, I found the popular TV show, The Amazing Kreskin, fascinating to watch partly because many of his performances could be explained rather easily if one knew what to watch for and where and when to look. That is not to say the things he did weren't real. But if they were, there were much easier ways to do them than by being a mentalist.

I decided taxidermy might be a way to fill my need for recognition and fame. I enrolled in a mail-order course, invested in some glass eyes and excelsior for my specimens, and a nose plug for me. I needed dead things for mounting. It was near the end of World War II and ammunition was a scarce commodity. I learned to trap small animals and developed considerable skill with a 22-calibre rifle. I would take one bullet with me and hike out to the patch of trees a short distance away to acquire a specimen. I'd have to wait until I had found a nice looking specimen of some not too desirable bird or animal (like a gopher, crow, or magpie). Then I would wait patiently for a good clean shot. I rarely came back empty handed.

The whole taxidermy process itself was high on the 'yucky' scale and was never in the running as a long-term career goal for me. It was a useful experience for several reasons. I learned a lot about birds and animals and developed respect for them and their environment.

One unexpected thing I learned was that I was not afraid of death. One day, I was hunting, and being in a strange mood, I found myself with the rifle at my temple and my thumb on the trigger. I suppose it started with the idea I would shoot myself, but my overactive brain took over and I became engrossed in a conversation with myself. I wasn't sure I was brave enough to pull the trigger but the only way to prove that would be rather counterproductive to my knowing how brave I was. I certainly didn't want to chicken out, not that anyone would ever know. My internal conversation lasted long enough for me to end up sitting on a stump looking more like Rodin's 'Thinker' than a serious suicide attempt. I finally realized that if I didn't pull the trigger at that moment, I could work out the logic (or illogic) of the dilemma at some later time; but if I did pull the trigger at this moment I would never be sure if I did it just to prove a point—and I didn't have a clear idea as to just what point that was. That day, I returned home with the unused bullet and quit taxidermy forever.

I couldn't justify my having the power of life or death over a living creature (even myself) just for my own satisfaction, even if I rationalized the process as being one of preserving its image forever.

Life and death was an integral part of my existence on the farm from a very early age. The experience of chopping off a chicken's head and seeing it run around headless and spurting blood was as frequent then as it now is to visit the local supermarket to purchase an antiseptically prepared chicken for Sunday supper. Because I was a good shot, and pigs have very small foreheads, it became my job to initiate the first step in the slaughtering of pigs. Since I was good at that, I soon became the unofficial animal executor on the farm. We were spared no details of the skinning and preparation of carcasses for our daily food.

In later years, I became adept at counseling suicidal individuals and I've never lost one. I think my suicide counseling success was due at least in part, to my firsthand experience with the death of animals and my realization of just how easy it is to live or die.

I believe many suicidal young people just need to find something else to do or think about at that specific time . . . and maybe someone to really listen to what they have to say, no matter how long it takes. This might help explain why attempted suicides often are not repeated. The person is hospitalized for a period of time and has a totally new environment in which to sort out confusing thoughts, often unrelated to the apparent cause of the attempt. I used to be bewildered as to how a few hours in a hospital bed could keep a person from just going out and attempting it again. Maybe it has something to do with people attempting suicide as a way of getting other people's attention. Sometimes it takes a lot to get attention. Most attempted suicides are rather feeble attempts, probably with little real expectation of success. But they do get attention.

I thought maybe I would feel more fulfilled if I became some sort of sports hero. Hockey was out because it was Saskatchewan in the 50's and there wasn't a surplus of water to make skating rinks. Even the Swift Current Creek was bone dry by midsummer.

I had no ability or interest in team sports. In fact, I used to dread the Friday afternoons when the teacher would give the class a 'treat' and allow us to play baseball all afternoon. I alternated my time between hoping no one would hit the ball anywhere near me when I was in the outfield, and hoping I could at least hit the ball somewhere when I got up to bat.

I did feel that sports were an important part of life, for reasons I still don't understand. So I tried track and field. I wasn't too bad at high jumping, but I hated the trip down, and pole vaulting was just plain scary. Sprinting required too much concentration on the starting blocks. The starting pistol mostly startled me into forgetting I was supposed to start running.

Long distance running seemed to be a good choice. I could run laps in the gym at noon hour or after school, and on the roads at the farm every morning and evening. Besides, I could shower at school with hot and cold running water.

At home there was a large cistern in which water, trucked in from somewhere, was stored. Water was hand-pumped out of the cistern and heated on a coal stove. There was a bathtub upstairs so the heated water had to be carried in pails up to the tub. It was quite a major process. The bathwater would flow down the drain, through a pipe and out into the yard. In the summer it was easier to use a washtub in the yard.

My father often said, "Get outside and get the smell blown off you."

At the time, I thought it was just a funny way to say, "Go get a breath of fresh air." Maybe he actually exactly what he said.

My running eventually produced painful shin splints on the sides of my legs so I had to give up running. It wasn't a big sacrifice because I hadn't managed to break the five-minute barrier at a time Roger Banister was running the four-minute mile. I had to accept that my future fame in the world lay somewhere else other than sports.

In class, my friends and I had a lot of spare time. We used to practice throwing our geometry compasses so they would stick into the floor or walls. We got really good at it and threw them into the floor with great enthusiasm. One day I was sitting with my legs sticking straight out into the aisle while my friend was flipping his compass near them. I'm not sure if it was his bad or good aim that caused the compass to suddenly be sticking into the bone of my leg. It didn't hurt, but neither of us was sure what the protocol was for removing a compass from a leg. Tentative pulling on it indicated it was well imbedded. Discussing it with the teacher or anyone in authority was not an option because that could easily lead into discussion as to how such an interesting event had occurred. So I held my leg firmly while my friend grabbed the compass with both hands and pulled it out.

Everything seemed alright until I noticed my sock getting wet and red. Pulling up my pant leg revealed a little rivulet of blood running down my leg into my sock. I stuffed a hanky up my pant leg and it stopped the bleeding. This was my first revelation that I was actually defenseless against random damage at the hands of the world. Prior to this time I worked under the assumption, as I think all teenagers do, that I was invincible, invulnerable, and indestructible.

Later that same summer another event shook my feelings of eternal security. Working on the farm with machinery and cars I had somewhere picked up the feeling that people my age never die. I think I have mentioned earlier that I make no claim to ever being smart. Safe procedures and caution were not part of my way of life. If a car was up on a jack I just naturally assumed it would stay there. Why should it fall over when I was under the car? Just because the power takeoff from the tractor to the combine was spinning a few inches from my pant leg, why should that concern me? If the pickup on the combine was blocked, why waste time and effort stopping it before I reached in to unplug it?

That summer, I learned that a school friend of mine had been killed while riding in the back of a pickup truck when its load of lumber shifted. Fortunately for me, this occurred when school was out and I didn't learn about it until well after the funeral. What bothered me most was that he had asked to borrow some money from me before school closed and I had turned him down. And now it was too late. I still have great difficulty in rejecting a request for financial help even from total strangers on the street.

I discovered in my teen years I have a tendency to step off roofs. I was painting the shingled roof of a small shed with brilliant red, oil-based paint. After painting for a couple of hours, I was a bit bored and stood up to stretch. The roof looked so nice I decided to get a better look and stepped back for a better perspective. It did not occur to me that the nice expanse of painted roof stretching out in front of me might imply I was close to the edge of the roof. I ended up draped over a gasoline storage tank with the half-gallon of red paint upside down on my head and running down over my chest. My mother was horrified when she saw me because she thought it was blood. This scenario was repeated on another occasion many years later, off a garage roof into a water barrel. This time it was water-based paint, which was a definite improvement. And it wasn't red.

I have developed the habit of talking to myself whenever I have to work on a roof, "Don't step back, you are on a roof, don't step back."

***

~ *The Argument Continues* ~
(from a September 2008, news report)

About 100,000 American horses are exported for slaughter in Mexico and Canada each year.

The U.S. 'Prevention of Equine Cruelty Act,' would make it a crime punishable by up to three years in prison to possess or transport horsemeat for human consumption or horses intended to be slaughtered for human meals.

School Daze

School was very easy for me and astonishingly boring. Sometimes I didn't get really good marks because I forgot to pay enough attention to know what the topic was, or I didn't pause to figure out what the teacher would expect to be the correct answer. Often my ideas were different from those of the teacher . . . or of the rest of the world, for that matter.

I don't remember much about my years in the elementary grades. Mostly, I think I stayed out of everyone's way and they stayed out of mine, with the exception of two incidents that I remember. One was when a friend of mine was picking a fight with me and wouldn't leave me alone. I put him in a headlock, with his head under my arm, and punched him in the face three times in rapid succession and then let him go. He was surprised but not really hurt. There wasn't even any blood. I think he had been expecting some pushing, sparring, and light punching, but I couldn't be bothered with that sort of thing. We continued to be friends, but he paid more attention to what I was saying after that.

The other incident occurred when I was at a urinal doing my business. Another student I didn't know, but remember him as being older and bigger, came up behind me, pushed me and told me to hurry up. I wheeled around and told him to leave me alone. He swore at me and disappeared to try and get himself dried off. I turned back and continued emptying my bladder. It may not have been the best way to make friends, but I didn't get teased or bullied . . . at least not twice.

Don was a fellow in my grade through high school who always wanted to come and visit the farm. He loved the open spaces and besides, I had an archery bow and a dozen arrows. We would shoot the arrows as far away as we could and then try to find them. We would do this until we ran out of arrows and had to find something else to do. During the days after he left, I would slowly recover most of the arrows, and by the time I had found them it would be time for him to come and visit again.

For a couple of years, a lot of my spare time was spent reading everything I could find about perpetual motion machines. My research got a huge boost the time I read an 'Unforgettable Experience' in the Readers Digest. It described in detail how a person got trapped in an underground tunnel by a water flood. The tunnel came to a blind end with a solid wall of water blocking the open end. The writer was trapped in the air space between the solid dirt wall on one side and the solid wall of water at the other end. This to me was a perfect model for a perpetual motion machine. All one would need is a paddle wheel half-in and half-out of the water wall and it would spin forever. I tried a few small experiments but couldn't manage to create the necessary vertical wall of water because gravity kept pulling it down. I didn't have the equipment necessary to dig a big horizontal tunnel. I did think of using a gopher tunnel. We had lots of those at home, but I would have needed such a very small paddle wheel. I wrote to the Readers Digest for more information on the article and/or author. To their credit, they replied honestly. Unfortunately, the news was that they did no research on articles submitted and took no responsibility for the truth of them. I don't suppose they noticed, but their readership immediately went down by one. I was disillusioned with them.

A few times I hit roadblocks in school that seemed insurmountable. One was at the end of Grade 6. I was advised that I wouldn't pass to junior high until I memorized the multiplication table up to the 'twelve times' table. For some reason, probably psychological or attitudinal, the information just would not stick. I spent a miserable first month of the summer holidays trying to memorize the table but couldn't get past the 'six times' tables. Then one day I had an epiphany. I could multiply in my head by two very easily. So, eight times seven (a total impossibility for me to memorize) was the same as twice four times seven. Four times seven was easy, and that just left me with simply multiplying by two. If both numbers were odd (like nine times seven) it took one more step. Just subtract one from one of the numbers to make it even, divide that number by two, use the memorized table in my head to multiply the numbers together, then double the answer and add the other number back onto it. Now, isn't that easier than memorizing a bunch of unrelated facts? It was for me and I finally passed into junior high.

Fortunately for me, the teachers never caught on that I couldn't learn the alphabet either. I could recite it by rote but had no idea what letter came before or after another unless I took a run at it from the beginning. I even learned to recite the alphabet backwards, but that didn't turn out to be very useful. I still can't find a letter in the dictionary without taking a run at it. I have improved in that I don't need to start from 'A' I only need a few letters lead. Lucky for me the teachers didn't clue into this or I'd probably still be in Grade 6.

Getting out of Grade 9 presented an unexpected problem for me. I had a straight 'A' report card, but at the end of the year I was late in handing in my Art project. I told the teacher I had it done (which I did) and would hand it in as soon as I could. The teacher advised me that if I didn't get it handed in the next morning I would fail Art and not get into High School. Not wanting to take the chance that I might forget to bring it to school the next day, I solved the problem rather simply. I told her I was not handing it in tomorrow or ever and she could fail me if she wanted to have me in her class for another year. In retrospect, that was maybe not the smartest course of action. I'm not sure how it all played out, but it didn't involve me anymore and I was passed into High School. It wasn't as if Art were a major subject except in her mind. I wondered what world she was living in.

So much for my first nine years of school—high school turned out to be much the same.

History was a major pain in high school because I couldn't memorize dates. Well, that's not quite true. I had no trouble memorizing the actual dates. I just had trouble remembering which dates went with what events.

One of the highlights of my high school career was our school brass band, organized and led under the long-suffering baton of Mr. W. I had taken a few piano lessons when I was in elementary school but they were not very memorable for me. They may have been more memorable for my teacher because I had absolutely no sense of rhythm, couldn't carry a tune, kept hitting the wrong keys, and was probably less than an ideal student in ways I have mercifully forgotten. At any rate, I discovered that I could play the trumpet. It had only three valves to push, so that was much easier for me to keep organized than with the 88 of a piano. I played the trumpet in the band for a year before I discovered that its sound was, to put it mildly, strident. I was more of a mellow person, so I switched to the coronet (a softer tone but still shrill), alto (uninteresting music), trombone (no way—the slide would provide me with an infinite choice of inaccurate notes), and tuba (really boring *'oom pah pah'* music). I even tried the clarinet, but the reed always seemed to need adjustment. Even then, it would often squawk in a most embarrassing manner.

Then I discovered the euphonium, and it was love at first sound. Euphoniums come in a variety of types depending on the design. Check the Internet with Google for way more conflicting information than you could ever want: three-valve or four-valve, baritone or bass, one or two bell. The euphonium has the most magnificently mellow tone imaginable, and the music written for it features obligato passages, which wander and float around the main musical theme with reckless abandon while the band plods along with the melody, harmony, and bass. The euphonium is often featured in a cadenza, in which everyone (including the conductor) stops to give the euphonium player full freedom to do his/her own thing with an extended passage. The euphonium lends itself to the elaborate variations written originally for trumpet or even violin (such as 'Carnival of Venice' and 'Flight of the Bumble Bee'. Check 'YouTube' for some magnificent performances by David Childs.

The euphonium was never as popular in North America as in Europe (except for military and marching music) and is relatively unknown in jazz or orchestral music. It seems that many composers are under the impression the slide trombone can fill in adequately for the euphonium and has the added value of having the slide for glissando musical effects. The latter part is true. The baritone sax provides a more focused sound appropriate for jazz. A well-played euphonium fills the room with sound—not a desirable quality in jazz.

I threw myself into my music with an enthusiasm that was borderline obsessive, practicing at least two or three hours every day, and always with a metronome. I learned to transpose music from any key and clef to the euphonium's key of B-flat. Initially, I wrote the transpositions by hand but quickly learned to transpose by sight. Music had become my claim to fame. I was technically great, had great tone and expression, and could play almost any music written.

When marching was added to the band's repertoire, I discovered I had another problem. It wouldn't have been so bad if they had just done ordinary, straight down the road, marching, but they soon decided to get fancy and do formations and patterns as we went down the road. And then we started doing a few intermission shows, which embodied fancy formations on a playing field. I couldn't remember which was my left foot and which was my right one. Drill sergeants are very fond of saying, 'left foot' or 'turn right'. This was a problem for me because I wasn't great at this kind of multi-tasking. Playing and marching was quite enough without having to figure out which was my left and right. I solved the problem by realizing that I was right handed. So, I could just clench my writing hand (or pinch my pant leg) and I knew which was my right side. That helped me immeasurably.

The school band helped me personally in that I was part of a group and traveled to other cities for festivals, concerts, and events like the Calgary Stampede. We did have impressive uniforms, which we wore for stage performances as well as marching. Somehow the uniforms were never as much of a chick magnet as I had hoped. Maybe the plumes on the hat were a turnoff. I frequently played solos and won competitions. Sports had proven hopeless for me and academic success was an empty achievement because I didn't see any use for it. Music was a recognized achievement that maybe could become my future.

After one festival, the adjudicator suggested I apply for a musical scholarship to study music and become a professional musician. I was excited . . . until I realized I had absolutely no real talent for music. I was functionally tone deaf and had to tune my instrument by listening for interference 'beats'. I had no natural sense of rhythm—just a memorized metronome beating in my head. What the adjudicator had seen and thought was talent to be developed was actually the end result of all my hard work. I was as good as I was going to get, and I needed to accept it.

The euphonium never became my destination but it remained a major part of my journey throughout university life. It was a great journey and helped me maintain some semblance of sanity.

Throughout my high school years (and sporadically during later years) I was active in amateur plays. My first experience was as the drunken choir director in Wilder's 'Our Town'. This was a memorable experience for me for several reasons. It was the first time I had acted on stage in a formal play, as opposed to acting as a magician or a brass band member. Goodness knows, I had done lots of impromptu acting in school classrooms over the years, and I was comfortable being on stage performing euphonium solos, but this was the first time I became a totally different person in front of an audience.

I was particularly pleased to get good reviews for my drunken acting role because I'd never even had an alcoholic drink up to that time, and probably had never seen a drunken person, as far as I can remember. I guess I just had natural ability as a drunk. The teacher directing the play arranged for a professional acting coach to work with us for one session. I had no idea how emotions (real or not) could be conveyed through techniques such as changing the pitch of your voice as you go through a long speech. It is more effective than changing the volume, and the two together can be electrifying.

The message of 'Our Town' that the love between human beings is divine, but we go about our lives trampling on the feelings of those around us, had a major effect on my developing philosophy and understanding of life. It is a great play.

***

~ One Of Ken's Crazy Arithmetic Systems ~

Ken: "I liked addition much more than subtraction.
I couldn't easily subtract 8 from 35, but 8+2=10 (obviously).
So add 2 to 35 and then simply subtract 10 to get the answer 27."
Simple, eh?
(That is a rhetorical question.)

IT'S NOT WHERE YOU'RE GOING

kevin millikin

IT'S HOW YOU GET THERE

Kevin Millikin

My First University

University was my escape route from our small, marginal farm in Saskatchewan. It was a good place to go after high school. Both my parents were university graduates—my mother graduated in Home Economics from Guelph University in Ontario, and my father from the University of Manitoba in Agriculture. It was easy for me to sell the idea of going to Manitoba, and it would get me far enough away to rule out frequent trips home. What else could I do? I graduated at the top of my class but didn't have a clue about jobs or careers or anything about the world. So, of course I went to the University of Manitoba. I invented plausible reasons to go to university in sunny Manitoba instead of bleak Saskatchewan without planning far enough ahead to realize that all the scholarships for which I could have applied were only available if I stayed in Saskatchewan. As I have said, I was good in school. I never said I was smart.

My first problem was to decide in what faculty I should enroll. Agriculture was not an option. I had not enjoyed my 16 years on the farm. Engineering was a bad idea because my brother was taking Engineering. The faculty of Arts was a possibility but it seemed to be a bit vague. I had nothing against Science, so it seemed like the best option. And thus did I choose my goal in life, or so I thought at the time.

I gathered up what money I could, applied for every 'teacher assistant' job listed in the university information and headed off for life in the university residence. Residence provided food and lodging at a reasonable price and it was right there on the campus so it was convenient. Besides working in three science labs to make ends meet, I quickly discovered that my ability to play the euphonium was not only a saleable skill, but also one that was in considerable demand. I joined the Reserve Army Winnipeg Grenadiers as a member of their brass band and attended practices at the Minto Barracks once a week for a rather good monthly wage plus extra for parades. It more than paid my room and board. Fortunately there were no wars during that time or I might have found myself in Afghanistan playing with a rifle instead of a euphonium. Probably I should have checked into what could have been expected of me as a member to the Reserve Army. I suppose the uniform and drill parades should have been a clue.

By the end of my first year I was also being paid to play in two other brass bands. Band practices and performances took up many evenings. I was spending three afternoons a week working in labs, evenings and weekends checking lab books. After my first year, I was on the student council as coordinator of musical programs in charge of reviving the defunct University Marching Band and promoting performances of the University Symphony Orchestra, student dances, and other musical activities. It was a busy life with no problems.

I never did get the hang of going to classes. I didn't learn well by listening and there didn't seem to be all that much to learn anyway. A few hours in the library seemed to more than cover everything (except advanced Organic Chemistry—it always made my head go in circles). As long as I had a friend in the class to give me the assignments and to tell me when the exams were scheduled it was easy enough to get A's.

Once I misread the exam schedule and went to the wrong building. This shouldn't have been such a big deal, but I somehow felt I was caught in the classic donkey between two bays of hay situation (except in my case, my choices were equally bad). As you probably know, the story is that a donkey was equidistant between two equally attractive bales of hay, and starved to death because he couldn't decide which one to eat.

I was caught between deciding whether to hustle over to the other building and go into the exam late (we had 30 minutes of leeway to enter the exam room) and face the disdain of my friends, or to go home and then have to write the exam another time. It wasn't a big decision—maybe it was that the decisions were equally unimportant. Being somewhat more intelligent than a donkey, I didn't just stand there until the clock made my decision for me. I went to the student coffee house to work out my situation. In effect, I had stepped away from the problem and could look at the big picture. Obviously, the only logical decision was to write the exam and not care if people made fun of me for being late. I wrote the exam, and finished earlier than most of the others even with my late start. My friends were impressed with my level of confidence in not worrying about getting to the exam on time.

My biggest problem on exams was more from not knowing what the professors expected as answers, than in learning the actual material. For instance, I almost failed a Physics class in which the professor made errors in almost every proof he gave in class. I didn't know that because I missed classes and unwittingly gave the correct proofs from the text when I wrote the exam. He marked them as being wrong because they weren't what he had given in class. When I wrote the supplemental exam, I gave two proofs for each question clearly indicating one as what he gave in class and then the other as the correct proof. I assume he was not amused because I got exactly 50%. I guess he must have marked his proofs as correct and the text ones as wrong.

Life in the university residence provided a ready pool of potential friends, some of them almost as naïve and unworldly as I was. Most of the foreign students stayed in residence at least for the first year and provided me with my first vista on the real world. My life in high school had been totally devoid of contact with people other than WASPS (White Anglo-Saxon Protestant). When I started university I knew nothing of sexual behaviors, social behaviors (legal or otherwise), or typical teenager high jinks outside the classroom.

Initially students in residence were arbitrarily assigned a roommate and then left to sort out the inevitable compatibility problems. It didn't take long for Len and me to gravitate into becoming roommates, sharing a small room with a set of bunk beds and two small desks. We were probably an unlikely pair. He was an Engineering student and I was in Science—not faculties that had a lot of love or outward respect for each other. According to Science students, Engineers learned how to do things but didn't understand anything; according to Engineering students, Science students knew a lot of theory but needed experiments before accepting even obvious information and then didn't know how to do anything with it once they had the information.

Len's view of academic achievement was that if you got anything more than a passing grade on an exam it meant you had been wasting time studying too much. My attitude was that if I got anything less than an 'B' then there was something wrong somewhere because I could get an 'A' in almost anything, if I wanted to, with a minimum of studying. We did have at least two things in common. We didn't study much and we both liked cars. His family even owned a classic Studebaker—the one that looked the same going backward as forward. I assume his interest in cars was inherited.

Len and I did share an abnormal interest in sports cars although his was in wanting to put a bigger engine into them (typical Engineer wanting more brute power) while I was more interested in the area of handling and racing abilities (the finer details). We also both found the residence meals to be unsatisfying and soon moved out into a small rented apartment. I learned to roast a chunk of beef tenderloin with vegetables around it, which became a weekly staple, and would last for several days. We still keep in touch even today.

I did have one professor whose classes I always attended. He taught Chemistry, had an honorary degree in English, had published humorous books and had a realistic outlook on life. In particular, I liked his attitude toward compulsory attendance.

At the beginning of the year he announced, "I am required to take attendance regularly and I will . . . on the first class of each month."

And he did. For most of his classes he would begin by asking if we wanted to discuss Chemistry or something else. Usually he discussed other topics we suggested. He maintained, as did I, that Chemistry could best be learned from a text, in front of a fireplace, in the evening, with good music, and with a cool drink. What we learned about life from him could not be learned from any book . . . unless it was one he had written.

There was another professor who earned my respect (but I rarely attended his classes). One time, a friend gave me the assignment from his class—due the next day by the time I got it. The assignment was to explain concisely what message the poet had been trying to convey by his rather long and convoluted poem. I'm not sure from where my inspiration came, but I found that if I took the last letter of each line and used it as the beginning letter of some appropriate word it would spell out sentences explaining his poem. I took this idea and expanded it with appropriate verbiage and handed it in. I was only hoping to get a passing grade on it and avoid a 'black mark' for not completing the assignment.

I was amazed to get an 'A' with a comment I have never forgotten: "I don't agree with a single thing you have said. But I would hate to try to argue against it."

At last I felt I had found a kindred spirit who recognized that regurgitation of previously learned knowledge should not be the only goal of a university education. He accepted the journey as more important than the final result. I have sometimes had the passing thought that maybe a person could do the same thing with any poem, but I've never taken the time to try it. I prefer to think I had stumbled upon a secret message from the poet written just for me in my time of need.

At the end of my first year, my Physics professor talked me into taking Honors Physics. I think he was impressed that in solving problems I would always derive the equations on the exam (this was in the olden days when students were expected to have memorized the equations). Little did he know that I could never memorize them correctly, and so deriving them was the only way I would have them. I went for the combined Honors Physics and Math program mostly because I had no idea what else to do.

There was only one course, Basic Concepts of Mathematical Analysis, which I totally didn't understand. No one in the class knew what Dr. M. was trying to do, why he was doing it, or how he was doing it. He would walk into the class, glance up at us to see if there was anyone there, and then, without saying a word, pick up the chalk and begin filling the chalkboard with equations. He would add and subtract Greek letters purporting to prove something. The most disturbing thing about his lectures wasn't that we had no idea what he was doing; it was that we never even knew when he was finished. Every day, about three-quarters of the way through the class time, he would put down the chalk and walk out of the classroom without comment (he hardly ever spoke). Sometimes he would return, pick up the chalk, and carry on from where he had left off. Sometimes he wouldn't come back until the next day, in which case we would assume he was starting a new example.

One of the students knew that Dr. M had a penchant for doing card tricks, and every day would put an open deck of cards on his desk. Day after day, Dr. M. would come in, glance around the room, look at the cards and launch into his furious chalk work on the board. Then one day, he picked up the chalk, then put it down, turned and picked up the deck of cards. He took a few cards in each hand, and without saying a single word he went through a long series of movements. He moved cards from one hand to the other, showed a card and then another, and dealt them into two piles on his desk. Then he would do the same thing again . . . and again. I couldn't keep track of whether the cards he showed each time were the same each time or different.

After a while he put the deck back on the desk and began writing symbols of the chalkboard. I couldn't believe it. It was just like his lessons. I didn't know what he was trying to do or whether he actually did it, let alone knowing how he did it. We never left a deck of cards on is desk again.

His final exam began with the instruction, "Do not attempt more than 6 of the 8 questions."

The questions were of the type: "If (unintelligible mathematical letters and symbols), then prove (more of the same letters and symbols in a different but equally unintelligible order)."

I started writing the exam, adding and subtracting symbols and Greek letters as fast as I could. I gauged my time so I would have answers for 6 of the questions. I thought that quantity might offset lack of deep Mathematical insight. And yes, I did just as he did in class. I wrote symbols as fast as I could, and when the allotted time for a question was up I just quit right where I was and went on to the next question. Maybe I succeeded in breaking the code because I passed the course. Or maybe it was based strictly on quantity. I have no idea.

After one year in the program I switched out of it because I discovered that it consisted of nothing but Mathematics and Physics. You'd think someone would have told me! Did I mention that I wasn't very swift on picking up on subtle hints . . . like the name of the program? 'Honors

Math and Physics' should have been a clue, but I missed it. I was told that while a lot of students dropped out of the program because it was too rigorous or difficult for them, I was probably the only one to leave the course with good marks. Several people told me I was crazy to drop out because it would lead to a good job. I didn't dispute I was crazy, but I needed a wider variety of subject matter. I didn't want to end up knowing nothing but Science and Math and I wasn't enjoying the journey getting there. So I left the Honors Math/Science program and returned to the general Science program to pick up Arts subjects. I took Astronomy, Psychology, Chemistry, Philosophy, and English to complete my Science degree. I had way more Physics and Math credits than needed at the time, but I did find a way to use them many years later.

Having got into a less time demanding program, I found myself on the student council as Science rep. I also had more time to embark on projects such as getting uniforms for the brass band and to enlist the services of a qualified, experienced conductor. He was a real lifesaver for the band and for me. The uniforms were in the university colors of brown and gold and had appropriate peaked caps, very much like the Royal Canadian Mounted Police (RCMP) uniforms of that time.

After I graduated, I took a teaching job at Swan River with a plan to make enough money so I could return to university for my master's degree.

I really thought I knew where I was going.

***

~ No Prejudice Here ~

My friend Abby (Nigerian, I think) and I are trying to find a place for him to live other than the university residence.
Renter: "I'm sorry he can't stay here."
Me: "Why not? Are you prejudiced against him?"
Renter: "Oh, no. Not at all. I have no problem with your friend."
Me: "Then what is the problem with renting him the room?"
Renter: "It's the other people living here. They wouldn't like it."
Abby spent all his university years in residence.

***

~ Dress Up Time ~

I was driving myself and four other band members to a major concert event. As usual, we were late and I was hurrying. Suddenly there was a police cruiser pulling up beside me (they didn't use sirens and flashing lights much in those days).

Just as he pulled up beside me I put on my band hat. He took one look and then waved for me to follow him.

We had a police escort (at an excessive speed) to our event.

He probably knew we were university band members, but it made a better story to believe that he thought we were police officers in an unmarked car.

***

~ You Did Say 'All' ~

The ad had said 'Winnipeg Symphony auditions, all instruments' so I presented myself, replete with euphonium, at the appointed time.

The examiner, eying the euphonium and me suspiciously: "Did you bring any music with you?"

Me: "No. I know the symphony doesn't normally use a euphonium, so I didn't know what you might want to hear. Any music is fine. Trombone, baritone sax, trumpet . . . or violin is always good."

I played the few assorted violin selections he handed me. He said some complimentary things about my musical ability and the fact they didn't have any present use for a euphonium. I went away happy. He was impressed by my performance.

I hope he had enjoyed it as much as I had.

*

Working In The Mental Hospital

I needed a summer job, and it being the 1950's when jobs were plentiful, the university bulletin board provided me with a ready solution. The mental hospital in North Battleford was advertising for summer help and it sounded like a nice change. I had never been to northern Saskatchewan and the pay was pretty good with room and board included. Besides, I knew nothing about mental illness except that I sometimes wondered if I were losing my mind, or if it was just the other people with whom I associated. This could be a good chance for a reality check (or should I say 'sanity' check?).

On the train going to my new job I had the leisure time to read about the job I had accepted. It sounded easy enough and pleasant enough except for the section concerning it being a 'hospital' with the intrinsic expectation that there would be patient care such as feeding and goodness knows what else that I didn't want to think about. I thought the rotating shift work schedule would be easy. University life had prepared me well for staying up late at night and sleeping during the day when required.

The hospital was outside the small city of North Battleford, near the bank of the North Saskatchewan River. The hospital consisted of an isolated clump of brick buildings nestled among forest and small farm areas. One section of the main building was for male patients and the other for female. The doors were always kept securely locked with only the permanent staff having keys. There were a few trusted patients who also had keys to open the doors when necessary. Temporary employees such as I did not have keys. I was initially insulted to think they considered mentally ill patients to be more trustworthy than I. Eventually, I realized they might have a valid point for thinking that. After all, mental health is only one facet of a person's character and personality.

Life for the staff at the hospital was *déjà vu* of my first year residence at university complete with community dining hall and smallish rooms but with two single beds—an improvement over the university bunk beds. One difference was that because my roommate and I were on different shifts we were rarely awake at the same time and place and never got to know each other, except for saying hello and goodbye as we passed on our way to and from our shifts.

Training consisted mostly of a sheet outlining the schedule of where and when to report for shifts. There was always at least one regular staff member on every ward so we learned the ropes as we went. When we were presented with an unfamiliar situation we would just ask one of the other staff members, or one of the more normal acting patients. This system usually worked well. In retrospect, I think the new assistants were probably scheduled to be on the easier wards first.

The staff residence was 100 yards (more or less) from the patients' hospital and was generally quiet at that distance. However, starting two or three days before a full moon there would be a gradual increase in the sound level until it become an unmistakable cacophony emanating from the hospital. On the actual day of the full moon the quietness returned. I was impressed with this verification of the forces of the moon on human life and behavior.

Up to this time, I had been studying Physics and Math and had never taken a single Psychology course. I was told that each separate ward held a different kind of patient, determined by psychiatric evaluation: psychotic, severely neurotic, schizophrenic, legally insane, medical, etc. Try as I would, I found it impossible to identify the 'class' of mental problem from the appearance or actions of the ward members. Every ward seemed to have a wide variety of erratic behavioral patterns, obsessions, compulsions, speech characteristics and manner of social interaction (or lack thereof). Although I could accept the label, and understand how it was determined, I could not for the life of me see how the label helped in understanding the patient or his treatment. It was more like the biological classifications of butterflies—useful to identify them and talk about them, but providing no depth of information or understanding about them.

Some twenty years after I left the hospital, I learned that, in fact, mental illnesses were distinguished by a classification of symptoms in the Diagnostic and Statistical Manual of Mental Disorders (DSM). In 1988 the DSM divided mental disorders into the following major categories: substance use disorders, schizophrenic disorders, paranoid disorders, affective disorders, anxiety disorders, somatoform (i.e., physical symptoms), and disorders of infancy, children and adolescence. Each of these categories was further divided into several subtypes with descriptive behaviors.

One big problem with this method of classification is that it is totally circular. The group of observable behaviors determines the classification of the mental illness; the named mental illness is then used as the reason for the behaviors. For example, a person who had a split personality would be classed as 'schizophrenic'. Then, if you asked why the person behaved as though he had two personalities, the answer would be, 'because he is schizophrenic'. This did not seem to be very useful from the point of view of a person who was used to the laws of science, which could be used for the prediction of changes caused by altering the circumstances.

Another big problem was that studies over the past decades indicated even professional psychiatrists are often not able to agree on the classification for a disturbed individual. The classification of their 'illness' seemed to me to be arbitrary and not very helpful. At the time when I was there (1950) a major distinction was made between 'neurotic' and 'psychotic' based on the severity of mental disturbance.

A common expression of the time summed it up as:

"A neurotic builds castles in the air; a psychotic lives in them."

Another way of expressing it might be:

"A neurotic suffers inwardly from his day-to-day problems; a psychotic inflicts his mental disorientation on others in the environment."

This was an easy way to distinguish the severity of the illness, but not very enlightening. During the fifty years since I was there, the terms psychotic and neurotic have fallen out of favor and are no longer employed as official psychiatric categories, although they are still used in general non-medical conversation.

When the patients filed through the courtyard on their way to the dining room many of them detoured out of their lineup to touch a spot on one of the stone walls. Many years of frequent touching had worn an indentation half an inch deep in the solid stone. I asked one of the permanent staff members what would happen if the person could not touch the wall. He suggested I should find out. So I waited until a relatively normal looking patient moved out of the line and headed toward the wall.

I intercepted him and said, "It's OK. You don't need to do that," as I gently guided him back to the line.

I walked with him, carrying on a one-way discussion as we went into the building, got our meals and sat at a table with a few other patients.

We started eating and I thought to myself, "Well, I guess it isn't such a big deal after all."

Then I noticed he was getting very agitated and had stopped eating. Suddenly he got up and headed for the door. I caught up to him and held him gently but firmly, suggesting he was safe and it would be alright for him to come back to his meal. That was a bad idea. He became progressively more agitated until it soon became evident that he would get out of the room any way necessary, including over my protesting body.

I watched him leave, thinking: "Now what do I do? I've really messed up this time."

In less time than it took for me to get my brain in gear, he returned, sat down beside me and started carrying on a normal (for him) conversation. I didn't need to ask him where he had gone or what he had done. There certainly would be no point in asking him why.

Later in my life, after I became a teacher, I came realize that one of the things teachers frequently say to errant students is, "Why did you do that?"

It makes good sense as a question until you realize that no one can ever answer it. The best one can do is to make up some plausible rationalization for what they did. No one really knows why he or she does something, any more than the mental patient did.

Have you ever noticed that when you are speaking, you don't know what you are going to say until you hear yourself say it? No one really knows what he or she is going to say until they say it. So, who is it that is speaking through you? Maybe it is the effect of TV commercials? And, are you actually doing the thinking, or do the thoughts just appear in your head from somewhere and you merely claim ownership of them?

There were several well-educated and intelligent patients who had for some reason been forced to trade respectable and good paying jobs for a life of aimless wandering in the hospital. On their good days most of them could carry on lucid and coherent conversations on subjects of their choice. Most had trouble focusing on topics suggested to them.

One of my earliest experiences was having a patient call me to the window and tell me to 'look out there'. After a few minutes of his gesturing and describing 'them', it dawned on me that I was trying to see the patient's hallucination.

I think the real clue came when he said, "They are hard to see because they are green and blend into the grass."

I met a few patients who thought they were some famous person. And yes, there was one who believed he was Napoleon in spite of being over six feet tall (most people think of Napoleon as being a bit on the short side).

On a tour of the female side of the hospital, I did see a case of catatonic schizophrenia. She was a girl in her mid-twenties, who spent her time sitting with her back to a wall, didn't make eye contact, and never spoke.

There was one patient, kept bedridden in a separate private room, who was in the late stages of syphilitic dementia. He had a large ulcerous open sore in his side. In order to be allowed into his room a face mask and full gown were required. I would also have liked a gas mask.

One middle-aged fellow was there for being severely alcoholic. He was fun to talk with because he loved to give details of his life. Unfortunately, his brain had been thoroughly pickled from alcohol and Demerol for many years, making the accuracy of his stories subject to question.

He would say things like:

"The police picked me up at noon for being drunk. I wasn't. I'd had a 26 of whiskey for breakfast and my friend and I, we killed a 24 of beer. I was feeling a bit nervous so I took a shot of Demerol just before they picked me up. I didn't actually start drinking until after I talked to them."

Most of his stories were variations on that theme.

I was frequently on the ward with a patient who liked to chat with me. One day he shyly brought up the topic of Mathematics. I admitted I had studied Math at university and he asked if I would like to see something he had been working on for the last many years. I said I'd be very interested. He scurried off and returned with a notebook filled with calculations of the roots of quadratic equations. He said he could give me the roots of almost any equation I suggested by looking it up in his hundreds of calculation tables.

I tried him with a few and checked his answer using the quadratic equation formula every Grade 12 student memorizes. Invariably, he was right. When he asked how I knew he was right, I showed him the formula and did a couple of examples for him. He promptly disappeared into his room and didn't come out for three days. Then he came out and gave me some more equations to solve. I assume they were the toughest ones he could think up. He watched carefully as I solved them and then disappeared into his room for a couple more days.

He never spoke to me much about Mathematics after that except to show me some pages of his original geometric theorems based on the postulates of Euclidian Geometry. His was similar but totally different. I didn't have much opportunity to study them, but they seemed logical, precise, and accurate. I cared enough to often wonder what would happen to all his notebooks when he died, but not enough to try to find out. Now I wish I had cared more.

The easiest ward was the one with the criminally insane. You know, the convicted murderers. After the initial shock of finding yourself surrounded by a dozen individuals who had absolutely nothing to lose by killing you on impulse, it was a piece of cake. The majority of them were totally sane. They just had a good lawyer who kept them out of jail on an insanity plea. Most of my time was spend playing pool or cards with them and chatting.

They called their favorite pool table game 'golf'. It was nothing like the clubs-and-green outdoor golf, and not even what you would find by an Internet search with Google for 'pool golf'. It consisted of one ball for each player plus the white cue ball. The goal of the game was to force the person following you to 'scratch' or to miss hitting his ball, by getting him 'hooked'. A scratch or missing contact with your ball counted as one point against the shooter. It was an ideal game for them because any number of people could play, and the game never ended. Whoever had the lowest score was winning. They had nowhere to go and I had nothing else to do. What a perfect game for us!

My least favorite was the hospital ward. I just knew I wouldn't like looking after people who were old or sick or both and I was right. Whether or not they were mentally unbalanced was irrelevant except for looking after their assorted medications and making sure they didn't fake taking the pills or trying to sneak extras for later use.

But the hospital ward was the worst when you had it on the graveyard shift. One popular explanation for this term is that between midnight and eight in the morning everything is deadly quiet: no one is moving, one's eyes won't stay open, and the brain goes numb.

It seemed to me that more patients died during the graveyard shift than during other shifts. My first action when taking over on the graveyard shift of the hospital ward was to assess each patient to determine if he seemed likely to live until the end of the night. And if not, try to figure out if there were some way to get him through at least to the end of my shift. If someone died on the shift, it was part of the attendant's role to prepare the body and plug the body orifices. The first time this happened it was shocking to a person who had, prior to this time, never even seen a human corpse. I was most grateful to my supervisor who took pity on me and looked after the task for me every time as necessary. He saved me a lot of nightmares.

One memorable person was a large, slightly overweight man about 60 years old who spent his time sitting motionless on the edge of his bed. His total food intake, twice a day, was a small glass of fruit juice and a piece of dry toast. I was told he had been living on this diet for several years in spite of it not being enough calories to keep a person alive, let alone maintaining an overweight body.

I am reminded of the boy in India, Ram Bahadur Bomjan, who apparently lives on nothing but air and light. There is even a name for it—breatharian—which is defined as a person who is nourished by light and has no need for food or drink. Shouldn't it be called a 'lightarian'? I have trouble believing the whole idea, but then, I'm a scientist type and not a philosopher type. There are a lot of things I don't know. If you check 'YouTube' it will give you some interesting information.

When I was a teenager, I was sent to spend a summer with my Uncle Harry who was a doctor in Calgary. It was interesting to go through the mountains, especially after living on the Prairies. He told me that he had seen patients die just because they decided not to live, even though there was no medical reason for their life to stop. I have also heard that it is not uncommon for a devoted spouse to die within a short time of the death of their partner. Maybe it is also possible for a person to stay alive through the exercise of will power, although I would expect there must be some definite limitations.

This was in the mid-fifties when electroshock was routinely part of the regimen for severe depression. It is currently coming back into favour now, under the more descriptive name of 'Electro Convulsive Therapy'. The patient was strapped to a sturdy table and had at least four attendants to hold his arms and legs firmly to control the convulsions. Left free, the violence of the convulsions could break a limb or the patient's back. Electrodes were attached, one on each side of the patient's head at the temple, and the electrical shock was adjusted so that he would lose consciousness and have convulsions lasting at least 15 seconds.

There was often the side effect of recent memory loss. In some cases it was actually a good thing if the patient lost the memory of recent events that were contributing to his depression. It was not a pleasant treatment to administer or watch. I can only assume that it was less pleasant for the patient. The vast majority of the patients strongly, and physically, resisted the sessions. I never looked forward to assisting with the sessions and I never saw a patient who did either.

***

- Being Original Is Not Always A Good Thing -

Psychology 101 professor: "Your essay on a new method of classifying mental illness is plagiarism."

Me: "I don't use the concept of psychotic vs. neurotic. Have you ever seen any classification even remotely like this before?"

Professor: "No."

Me: "Then how do you know it is plagiarized?"

Professor: "Because we don't expect first year students to write at this level."

Me: (not mentioning I'd worked the previous summer in a mental hospital), "I'm in my final year, not my first year."

Professor: "Then I'll give you a mark of 50% for it."

I accepted the mark.

Several years later I discovered that 'plagiarism' had been noted on my permanent university record.

Kev's Life Story
by Kev Millikin

IT'S NOT WHERE I AM GOING

IT'S HOW I GET THERE

~ THE END ~

My Life In North Battleford

On my first day in the dining room, I noticed two of the staff members looking at me and talking. They were dressed in white coats and looked as if they belonged—unlike me. I smiled back at them and they came over to sit with me.

The taller one introduced himself as John and asked, "Are you here for the summer?"

I replied, "Yes. You guys are permanent here?"

"Yep. I've been on staff here for 5 years. Dan here will finish his training this year and then he will be permanent."

Dan reached across the table and shook my hand, enthusiastically. "Are you getting settled in OK?"

"Pretty much. It looks like my roommate and I are on different shift schedules so I'm mostly on my own. So far we have just passed in the hall once."

"Dan and I are going to town tonight for a few drinks. You want to come?"

"Sure. That would be nice."

"There is no beer here at the hospital, unless you find someone's stash cooling in a toilet tank."

"We used to do that at the university, too."

The three of us and one of John's friends spent the night at the local beverage room in North Battleford sipping draft beer while they told me stories about their life and the operation of the hospital. Mostly I listened, basking in the warm feeling of having made three friends on my first day . . . and having cold draft to drink.

On the drive back, Dan and I were in the back seat of the car talking and laughing.

"Drive slowly," Dan called out to John.

That struck me as a bit odd, but I didn't think anything more of it until Dan put his arm around me and pulled me closer, with his hand on my knee.

"No, drive faster," I shouted to John.

He ignored my plea and I realized he knew what Dan was up to—probably way more than I did.

The trip back was spent mostly in keeping his hands off me and holding him far enough away from me so he couldn't kiss me. You need to realize that at this stage of my life I had necked with a few girls, but that was all. I was vaguely aware that there were homosexual people in the world, but I had never occurred that I would ever meet one, let alone be trapped in the back seat of a slowly moving car with one.

In fairness to Dan, I must admit he really didn't do anything scary. It was more that I didn't know what he might do or try to do. The several beers I had consumed earlier in the evening probably helped me to view the whole thing as kind of a dumb, but not really annoying, game. I would push him away and he would gradually sneak up on me again. It was a slow motion game of cat and mouse with me being the mouse. The realization that I had always expected to be the cat in any romantic situation made me realize I had spent too much of my life concerned with interaction between chemical compounds and too little time with the interaction of human emotions.

The next morning, I was awakened to find Dan standing by my bedside.

"How did you get in?" I mumbled sleepily.

"Tony (my roommate) let me in. I brought you your mail."

"Thanks," I muttered.

Dan handed me my mail and left as I dropped off back to sleep.

Again, the next morning . . . and the morning after that, the scenario was repeated, with Dan staying longer to talk and sitting on my bed beside me. I started sleeping with my arm across my chest just in case he tried to kiss me while I was asleep, but he never did—as far as I know. I came to realize he had a crush on me and he had accepted that I wasn't interested in him. After a couple of weeks of being awakened daily, I asked him to stop bringing me my mail. We remained on friendly terms but he began avoiding me rather than seeking me out. I was happy to have the 'male' delivery stopped.

Life was much the same as it would have been in any small rural town in northern Manitoba or Saskatchewan at that time. Working, eating and sleeping took up most of the day because there were no recreational facilities closer than those in North Battleford and you needed a car to get there. Fortunately, John and his car were usually available for evening fun whenever my shift work allowed, because he didn't work shifts. So we, and usually two or three other staff, would do the usual things people do: driving around, going to town for a snack, stealing a turkey for Thanksgiving dinner, going to a movie, and drinking beer. Oh, so you think stealing a turkey isn't a usual activity? You are probably right, but at the hospital it seemed everyone except me thought it was a great idea.

Being raised on a farm I had some first hand experience with turkeys and the process of getting one from the barn onto one's dinner plate. It is a much more complicated process than foreseen by their plan. The extent of the plan was to drive to a nearby turkey farm, sneak into one of the barns and snaffle a nice fat bird. Our total preparation for the escapade was to have an empty flour bag to carry the bird. Off the top of my head, I could think of a few possible problems such as:

- Our society has a convention of eating only dead and cooked meat—preferably without feathers. I doubted the cook at the hospital would be happy with our request to cook a squawking, wing-beating bird.

- Turkeys are not quiet when excited, and they excite very easily.

- Turkeys are possibly one of the most stupid things alive. A clap of thunder will panic them into rushing into one corner of the barn and smothering each other, or possibly us if we happened to have also chosen that corner.

- Oh, yes. And it is also most likely illegal.

My subtle protestations were politely ignored as we sped on our mission. John turned off the lights and we drove slowly and quietly halfway down the lane. The consensus was that it would be best, in the interests of concealment, to walk the last 100 yards. We got partway to our goal when we heard menacing barking from what sounded like several very large and really annoyed dogs. My training as a runner finally paid off. I was easily the first to get back to the car. Unfortunately, it was locked. After we regrouped in the car, we realized the dogs were probably tied up but still an effective deterrent. That night we ate our hamburger dinner without comment.

One day I developed a sore throat, which rapidly progressed to the point where I couldn't breathe or speak. Being in a hospital setting, there was easy access to a phlegm pump and lots of available beds. I spent a couple of days in the 'staff' room in the hospital ward. I hadn't seen Dan for a long time, but suddenly there he was at the foot of my bed.

"I have to change the sheets," he said in a most professional manner.

My eyes must have betrayed my panic at the idea of his stripping off the sheets and exposing me in my near nakedness and helplessness. I was having my first (and only ever) attack of homophobia. I was afraid, and it was only because he was homosexual—not from anything he had said, done, or was likely to do.

"Relax. It will be alright," he said gently.

I would have said something like, 'Yeah, right', but fortunately I couldn't speak.

He seemed to understand my irrational panic about having him see me exposed without a sheet. I would still have a gown on but I felt I needed more protection than that. I still don't understand my panic as well as he did, and he was right. As the professional nurse he was, he slid the new sheets onto the bed, rolled me onto them and pulled the old ones off without ever exposing me below the neck. I wouldn't have thought it possible, but for him it was fast and easy. At that moment I think I could have kissed him (figuratively speaking, I mean) in relief at his recognition and consideration for my feelings.

The phlegm kept increasing so it was decided I should be moved to a 'real' hospital in North Battleford. It would have to be a trip without the pump (they didn't have a long enough extension cord) but with shallow breathing, coughing gently, and not moving, I could get just enough air.

Fast-forward to the hospital admittance desk clerk saying, "Your Saskatchewan Health Insurance Card, please."

This presented a problem: I had Manitoba Health Insurance, but not for Saskatchewan, and even if I had insurance I wouldn't have had the card with me. I grabbed a pen and filled out the form with the first nine digits that came to mind. I sometimes wonder if they are still trying to match up someone to those numbers. I was hustled into a room with a cot, still wearing my hospital gown.

An official looking person in white peered at me, "What seems to be the problem?"

I gasped, choked, coughed and gestured to my throat.

"A hot compress should help that," he said.

I may not be a doctor, but I am pretty good with science and my best guess was that a hot compress would cause expansion of the phlegm and further close my throat. I shook my head negatively as emphatically as I could.

I regained consciousness in time to hear him say, "Humph. Maybe this cold compress will work better."

I realize now that I must have gasped and choked for at least a minute before losing consciousness, but I had absolutely no memory of that period of time—not even of his getting the compress or putting it on me. A similar thing had happened once before when I was a kid. I ran full speed into an iron pipe that caught me just under my nose, knocking me unconscious. I woke up flat on my back. There should have been some memory of my face hitting the pipe and the pain of hitting it, but my mind was blank for several seconds before the collision.

The cold compress worked well enough to get me moved onto a ward and into the bed I would call mine for the next ten days of tests.

John came to see me every evening and reported on what tests had been done and the lengthening list of negative results. As a last resort they did a spinal tap, which was excruciatingly painful. However, by this time my throat seemed to have decided to behave and I was functioning quite well. One evening, John smuggled in a bottle of beer for me, so I knew I must be alright. He would never have done that if I were still considered to be at risk.

The next morning I overheard a nurse remark, "He really slept well last night."

After that they stopped waking me up in the middle of the night to give me a sleeping pill.

By now I wanted to get out of the hospital. I had been told that I had a growth removed from my neck when I was very young, and I recall being kept home from school for a month or so with blood poisoning in my left arm, but this was the first time in my life I had been required to stay overnight in a hospital and I wasn't enjoying it much.

I suggested to the doctor I was well enough to leave. He wasn't too sure. I offered to hop out of bed and do ten push-ups for him as proof. He declined the offer, but did say I should be able to leave on Friday.

When Friday came, I told the nurse I was supposed to leave now. She replied that there was no order to that effect and the doctor had gone to his cottage for the weekend. That evening, John came to visit and heard my story. He found my clothes stashed away in a closet and brought them to me.

He and I left through the front door to the sound of the nurse loudly repeating, "You can't leave the building without the doctor's permission."

She was wrong. We could and we did. A couple of years later I had my tonsils removed and have never had a recurrence of my undiagnosed malady.

The rest of my term at the Mental Hospital was business as usual except for Dan.

One night, John told me Dan was in the hospital with severe internal injuries. It seemed, according to John, that a group of staff members took it upon themselves to lay in wait for Dan with a large sheet, fists, feet and baseball bats.

Dan recovered after a significant time in hospital. I am still sorry for not having visited him while he was recovering. I don't think it had anything to do with homophobia. John did suggest it might be wise for me not to be seen publicly with Dan any more.

As I was leaving the institution to return to university, Dan gave me a small gift and a card. I thanked him and we shook hands (I had still not learned to hug male friends) but I didn't look at it until I was back in the safe privacy of my residence in Winnipeg. It was a slightly mushy card and a set of cuff links—an appropriate gift for the mid-1950's when people wore shirts with cuffs. I wrote him what I thought, at the time, was a polite note of thanks but indicating we could never be anything but distant friends.

He responded with what I now know is called a 'hissy fit' note demanding the cuff links be returned to him. I sent them to him with a note of apology. I can only hope that I hurt him less by being honest than I would have by leading him on. I felt I had failed him as a fellow human being, but I didn't know what else to do at the time. I still don't how I should have handled it.

The hospital held dances periodically for the socialization of the male and female patients. Very rarely was there anyone from the outside world except staff at them, but it always surprised me how well the patients functioned in that setting. At one dance I got chatting with a fellow, named Sam, in his early 20's.

He seemed to be totally normal, sane, and sensible. He asked me how he could get out of the hospital. It seemed to be a fair question to me, so I said I could do some checking for him if I knew who was his psychiatrist. He didn't know because he said he hadn't seen one for the past 3 years.

I discussed his comments with John (my source of all information at this time). John said there was supposed to be an evaluation every year but he would look into it. In the meantime we should get to know Sam a bit better.

John and I took Sam for a night out. We played some pool, did some drinking, had burgers with fries, and talked a lot. Sam tried, without success, to pick up every girl he saw. We got back late to the hospital, but John knew how to sneak him back onto the ward unnoticed. I did wonder how it was that I got reprimanded for taking Sam out of the hospital, but it wasn't a big deal. Probably Sam had needed to tell someone about what a good time he had. John and I agreed Sam was probably saner than we were, so John pursued the project of getting a reassessment.

Within two weeks Sam had been discharged from the hospital. John told me afterwards that the assessment consisted mostly an interview enquiring into whether I had made any improper advances to Sam or had shown any interest in him sexually.

It is interesting to note this was 1954. It wasn't until almost 20 years later (1973) that the American Psychiatric Association removed homosexuality from its list of psychological disorders. I guess Sam and I passed that sanity test.

I did meet up with Sam after he had been released from the hospital. He was living on his parents' farm part way between Swift Current and Regina. I needed to get some machinery parts in Regina so I phoned him and asked if he would like to keep me company.

We had to put in a couple of days waiting for the parts to be available (or maybe that was just an excuse to spend a couple of days in Regina. My memory fails me on that point.) We stayed in a hotel, drank a bit, went to dances and behaved like normal young bachelors out on the town.

One night Sam drank way too much and was really drunk. He somehow managed to fall against the sink in the bathroom and severely bruised (probably cracked) a rib. I had heard stories about drinking yourself sober. Sam changed instantly from a staggering, word-slurring drunk into a clear-speaking sober-acting person. Even his brain seemed to work normally. We took a taxi to the hospital, got his chest taped up and came back to the hotel. He was still appearing way more sober than I was, but we decided the party was over for the night. Off the top of my head, I think this phenomenon is somehow the same as when a skilled typist or piano player goes into an 'automatic pilot' mode and can carry on a conversation while typing or playing. His brain just went into an automatic living mode.

I finished my stint at the Mental Hospital without further incident and returned to the University of Manitoba to complete my B. Sc. degree.

Death By Division

(Inspired by comments on a friend's death
from AIDS circa 1990)

Like a cuckoo's egg
In a robin's nest,
The invader hid as one among millions,
Stealing shelter and nourishment, unnoticed.

Biding its time
Waiting to strike.

A receptive disciple
And a swift conversion,
Now there were two, then four, then eight.

Increasing in galloping geometric progression.
A covert army
Collecting its strength.

One by one
But thousands at a time
Each converted cells saps my remaining strength
Until there is none left and my body dies.

But it is only my body . . .
Not my soul.

Graduation And Off To Swan River

My days back at the university were pretty uneventful. I picked up university life from where I had left off in the spring with the exception that I would take courses in subjects other than Physics and Mathematics to complete my degree. I took second and third year courses both at the same time in: Introduction to and History of Philosophy; Inorganic, Organic and Physical Chemistries; Fundamentals of Psychology and Applied Psychology. I also took fourth year Modern Physics and Calculus and Differential Equations just for old time's sake.

I discovered a few weeks before my university graduation ceremony that I was expected to give a speech. It was because I was 'Senior Stick' or some such title. Preparing for the speech made me realize that I didn't have a clue about what I was going to do for the rest of my life after I had packed my belongings into my metal suitcase and left the university campus.

A few hours of studying career information and listings of jobs available convinced me that a general Bachelor of Science degree was not the ultimate key to any long and satisfying career I could identify. It didn't even qualify me for a good temporary job. I had no marketable skills or useful experience. Everyone seemed to want 'previous experience'.

Then it hit me. The only thing I knew, and was good at, was going to university. I could become a professional student—otherwise known as a university professor. I would need some money for more full-time study and, as always, I was temporarily out of funds. The date was 1955 and Manitoba was so short of qualified public school teachers they were hiring university graduates as 'permit' teachers to teach in small rural schools. The $2700 a year salary wasn't great, but not bad for that era. It was the price of a new car in those days, so it was like maybe $27,000 is today. If I saved my money for the year, it would give me a good start on my master's degree without needing to have too many other jobs during the year. AT LAST! I had a goal for my life and a plan to make it happen. I knew where I was going. Or at least, so I thought.

Swan River was a nice town, a 5-hour drive north of Winnipeg. It had one high school with one class each of Grades 9–12. As luck would have it they were looking for a Science/Math teacher. It would be perfect for me, I thought, because I had majored in Physics, Chemistry, and Mathematics. There would be a few classes of fill-in subjects like Art and maybe some Physical Education classes but I knew I could handle them.

It somehow did not occur to me that my background in the field of education consisted mostly of skipping classes or ignoring whatever the teacher was doing. The only teachers I had paid attention to in school were the ones who were interesting because they didn't stick to the subject area. Of course I was ready to be a teacher. Bring on the students!

Most small cities at that time had room-and-board accommodation in private homes for the new teachers, ministers, or other unmarried transients. The one I found already had two young teachers staying there. The lady provided good meals, it was a pleasant atmosphere, and there was a pitcher and basin in the room for washing up. Occasionally, on the coldest winter mornings, there would be a thin layer of ice on the water in the pitcher. I had become used to this as a child and just took it as an effective way to ensure I was awake for school. There was a house rule that there would be no alcohol in the house. Being 21 years old and having only recently 'come of age' as far as buying liquor (and other adult activities), this was only a minor disadvantage for me. It became even less of a disadvantage when I discovered that she considered Guinness Stout to have medicinal benefits and was thereby exempt from the no-alcohol rule. I assured her that the reason it was sold at the local Liquor Commission was because it was manufactured in Canada by Labatt's Brewery. It was true enough and she found it reassuring. By the end of the school year I was very healthy (mentally and physically) but never did develop a taste for room temperature Stout.

I preferred the cold beer in the local hotel beverage room for two reasons. The first reason is self-evident—it was cold beer. The other reason is because of an unsolved mystery.

The first time I went into the beverage room and was served my cold beer the waiter refused payment with the comment, "It's paid for."

My second beer was also free; as was every one I had there all year. No amount of interrogation or subtle investigation brought me any closer to finding out who my unknown benefactor was. The beer arrived automatically as soon as I sat down regardless of what waiter was on duty, leading me to suspect the hotel owner. But it was only a suspicion unsubstantiated by any facts.

I prepared for my classes as much I could by going over the curriculum and making sure I knew the content I was supposed to teach. If I had been the one writing the exams I would have really aced those courses. My first few days of 'teaching' consisted of my demonstrating to the students that I could do the work while they watched in fascination at my skillful performances. I went over everything slowly, clearly and methodically, being careful not to make any errors. They copied down the work from the blackboard as instructed and no one asked any questions. I was confident that I was doing a superb job of teaching . . . until after I gave a couple of tests. The results were astonishingly bad.

One weekend, while quaffing my regular free beer, I realized that I was doing to my students exactly what Dr. M. had done to us in my Mathematical Analysis course in university. I was launching into diagrams and statements of proof on the blackboard without giving the students any idea of what I was doing or why. The only difference was that in my proofs there was a Latin notation, 'Q. E. D.' meaning, 'what was to be proven', so students would at least know when I was finished. My students knew when I was finished, even if they had no idea what it was that was finished.

On the following Monday, I embarked on a program of teaching WITH the students instead of AT them. When there was no real reason to learn something I would invent one:

"Wouldn't it be embarrassing if someone stopped you on the street and asked you what the molecular weight and valence of Aluminum was and you didn't know? You can avoid this embarrassment by memorizing it as 27 and plus 3."

I discovered that the weirder or more humorous the made-up reason, the easier it was for them to remember. I also learned from the world of advertising that frequent repetition of a simple fact or statement makes it memorable. I began starting and ending my lessons with a brief quiz or reiteration of important information.

I was not much older than the students I taught. I was 21 and Mavis was a well-developed 22-year-old who initially sat in the front seat of the middle row. She liked tight sweaters and frequently leaned back to stretch her arms. After the first two weeks I moved her to the back of the class directly behind a large boy. I'm sure she had no idea why I moved her . . . yeah, right.

There was not much formal entertainment in Swan River and no larger cities anywhere nearby. I had never taken an active part in team sports mostly because I was never a 'team player'. Whatever I knew about team sports was theoretical and gained by reading, or in a few instances, by observation. In fact, I have never owned or even put on an athletic 'cup'. The students were keen on sports but the staff was less interested in coaching and supporting them. What would be more logical than my volunteering to coach the school hockey team? I had never played hockey in my life so I knew nothing of the rules—let alone what a coach is supposed to do. The team said that didn't matter because they did. And I didn't know how to skate—obviously not a big problem for the same reason.

Once I got into the hockey business it was a short jump to serve as referee for basketball games. I read the rulebook and it all seemed pretty straightforward. Fouls and most things were obvious except for 'traveling'. It sounded so easy when I read it. The player must bounce the ball at least once for every step taken. Unfortunately, there was no way I could watch the ball and the player's feet at the same time as they raced from one end of the court to the other. In order to avoid rampant traveling by both teams I set up with a member of each team to give me the traveling sign if they saw a member of their own team traveling.

The students had an innate feeling for fairness and honesty. Besides, they knew I would verbally abuse them if they cheated. It was just all for fun anyway, not for championships.

I also got enlisted into being the football team's official 'medic'. Generally, it was an easy job once I learned how to tape up sprains and apply Band-aids. Fortunately, I had studied up on how to make stitches out of Band-aids, because in one game a player impaled his calf on a metal stake in the ground—in one side and out the other. The flow of blood was more impressive than the time I had a compass imbedded in my shinbone, but that experience reassured me I could handle the situation.

First thing was to decide what to do with the metal rod. Common sense told me that it would be best to leave it in his leg. However, the stake was also firmly anchored in the ground, so I gently lifted him and his leg off it. Except for the increased blood flow (and my sudden interest in throwing up my lunch) things seemed to be going well. I did a mostly adequate job of stopping the bleeding and fixing him up for his trip to the hospital. From there on it wasn't my problem. In those olden days one never even thought about lawsuits.

And speaking of lawsuits, I started an after school science club. Not knowing any better, I let the students choose the areas of study. They chose 'explosives'. To make a long story short, I obtained some fuming (that is one step more potent than concentrated) nitric acid from Winnipeg and we proceeded to make up a small batch of nitroglycerin—not something I had ever done at university. In the labs at university we made things like aspirin. I spent a number of sleepless nights wondering how we could explode our experiment in relative safety. As fate would have it, my worry time was wasted. One of the students spilled the 'brew' all over the lab desk. I used a rag to wipe it up. To the amusement of all of us, there was a trail of bright little popping explosions behind the rag as the diluted drops of nitro exploded individually. Everyone agreed the experiment had been successful and I decreed we should terminate the club in order to spend time on sports activities.

By the end of the year I was also umpire for the city adult softball team. The rules were more complicated than I expected until I caught on that the players didn't know (or at least, care about) some of the more esoteric rules, like invoking the 'infield fly rule' or the need to 'tag up' on an infield catch. That's the trouble with rulebooks—they don't say which rules are essential and which aren't. Some of my calls were surprising to the players (even if technically correct), but they accepted that I was better than nobody, and at least I was consistent. I suppose it might have helped if I had ever played softball or any kind of ball, for that matter.

There were many interesting students in the school. There was a pair of identical twin boys in Grade 9. They invariably dressed identically except that only one wore a belt. It was widely accepted that it was the same twin who always wore a belt and the other didn't. This made it very easy for the teachers to tell them apart and to identify them. We spent some time together in class and also after school. Eventually, I could tell then apart by their facial expressions. And then I discovered their secret. They would frequently switch the belt when it was more convenient for one of them to miss a detention than the other, or for some other reason, or just for fun. They admitted their deception to me and I promised to keep their secret. I was surprised at how often they switched identities for large periods of time, even for whole days.

Fortunately for me, the principal had no concerns about my fraternization with male students at recess or after school. He thought I was handling discipline matters on my own and saving him some problems. Besides, I helped fill out his extracurricular Physical Education program. It was really just that I preferred the company of the students who were my closer to my own age to the teachers who tended to be older and hence more boring.

I became good friends with three boys in particular: Mel, Jack and Al. Somehow, I'm not sure how, Al and I went on a 'field trip' by Greyhound Bus to Chicago during the spring break. He was planning to go to university in Vancouver when he graduated because his sister and her husband lived there and could provide room and board. He had spent his life in the sparsely populated area around Swan River and asked me about life in a big city like Vancouver. I don't know whose idea it was, but it seemed like a good idea to go to some big city. Winnipeg was handy, but not very exciting (or warm). We were both sick of winter and were suffering from a severe case of cabin fever. It wasn't exactly like spring break in Cancun, but it was warmer and the snow was melting in Chicago. We even got to hear Dean Martin perform in person, semi-drunk . . . him, not us.

The three of them were destined to play a major part in the next year of my life. After they graduated from Grade 12, the four of us set off to the University of British Columbia to live with Al's sister—them for their first year and me for my Bachelor of Education.

I think we drove non-stop from Swan River to Vancouver—something more than 24 hours. This would account for my lack of memory concerning the trip. The only thing I remember is the four of us constantly playing musical chairs to drive or to get a back seat for sleeping.

***

~ *Ouch* ~

It was my first day as the school hockey team coach. The students were changing and putting on their equipment.

I noticed one boy walking up to another and kneeing him severely in the groin.

My initial reaction was one of horror until I realized that was how they checked to see that their 'cup' was properly installed.

I never did learn not to wince every time I saw that.

Faculty Of Education At UBC

Jack, Al, Mel, and I found our way to the east side of Vancouver to the home of Al's sister (Evelyn), husband (Andy), and their young son. On the other side of the city was the University of British Columbia (UBC) where we were intending to enroll.

"Well here we are," Al said to his sister as the four of us filed into the house.

Evelyn was a relaxed, pleasant, self-confidant and attractive young lady. She smiled as she guided us to the kitchen table.

"Come in and sit down. I have a bite of lunch ready for you."

She looked at me, "You must be Bill. Al has told me all about you."

I got up and shook her hand, "Oh. I certainly hope not. Nice to meet you."

Jack had a permanent dark tan. I think from his surname he was maybe Ukrainian. He gave his usual half-shy, half-chuckling, deprecating grin as if enjoying a joke only he knew.

"I'm Jack," he said, looking down.

Mel was the good-looking member of our little gang. He was tall and thin with smooth regular dark features. He had a serious look, a quiet air of confidence and a beautiful singing voice, which he loved to exhibit in public. His eyes locked with Ev's. He grinned and nodded with just a hint of a wink as if they were sharing a secret thought. We never learned the secret, but had definite suspicions as the year went by.

"Andy will be home soon. Then we can take a run out to the university so you can see where it is. I hope you won't find it too crowded here. We have just the one small spare room and the two bunk beds fill it completely. But you have full run of the house."

We all agreed it would be fine, as we settled down to demolish the lunch, much to Ev's satisfaction.

Andy worked as a stevedore on the docks. He looked the part—big, sturdy and serious. The house showed the side benefits of his job. There were knickknacks and gewgaws everywhere, dishes of hard candy, wall ornaments—everything coming into Canada from overseas by ship that would fit easily into the game pocket of the hunting jacket he always wore to work. There was an easy but distant relationship among us. We respected each other, avoided arguments and only once hit a bump in our working relationship.

When my car needed a new tire I suggested since they were using the car they might contribute to the cost of the tire. One agreed with me; two disagreed. I don't even remember how this impasse was resolved or who was on my side. That's how little importance it was to our overall operation.

Andy was rarely around because he worked long hours and often into the night. Ships don't keep regular office hours. However, he made time to take us to a used car lot where he thought there was a good car for us (actually, more 'me' than 'us' since I was the only one with spare money). My first reaction to the car was not very positive. It was small, green and British.

My first question was, "How fast will it go?"

I wasn't looking for a racecar, but I did want one that would keep up with the traffic on the highway. The salesman assured us it would, and it wasn't expensive, so I bought my first of what would turn into a series of Morris Minor convertibles. I wish now I had kept one as a toy for my old age.

As the year went on, I learned of a racetrack in Abbotsford, about 45 minutes inland from Vancouver, where there were amateur races on the weekends. This was in 1957, and Chevrolet had upgraded their Corvette to a V-8 engine in 1955. There were a lot of people racing these new overpowered machines. It was fun to watch the Corvettes leave the other cars way behind on the straight stretches, and then get passed on the S-turns by Volkswagen bugs and even Morris Minors. It was surprising how many of the Corvettes would die in clouds of engine smoke a couple of laps before the end of the race.

I helped Jack with his Math (usually in spite of his reluctance) and felt we had a good, but distant relationship. During the first few months, Jack developed a close friendship with another fellow. Jack told me when it suddenly ended because the fellow was gay. I asked Jack why he couldn't have kept him as just as a friend because they always seemed to have fun and enjoyed doing things together. I didn't get any answer other than Jack's diverted eyes, shy grin, and an emphatic shake of his head. It didn't make sense to me then or now. I have several friends who are gay and we just have the same sexual relationship I have with straight men—none. It's just that simple.

A few years after I left Vancouver, I got an invitation to his wedding in Mexico. I tried to send a gift, but the address was a rental hall and I didn't know how to get it there on the right day for him to get it. That was the last I heard of him. Sounds ominous, doesn't it?

Al was a stocky, muscular, blond with a crew cut. I don't think I ever knew what he was taking at university but it seemed to go well for him. You may remember him from the beginning of this book as the fellow with whom I went to Chicago and who later ran off in my/his car to get married.

I have no idea what Mel was taking, or if he even went to university. I must have known at the time and have just forgotten. He was a great guy to have around because he enjoyed life and made sure it treated him well. He loved singing to any assembled group. One time in pub, he got up voluntarily and began singing. In a burst of uncharacteristic showmanship, I joined him and we sang together. He tolerated my presumptuousness with better grace than I deserved. But then, he was a really nice guy.

I had heard how wonderful it was to live in Vancouver, what with its warm winters and sunny summers. I was unprepared for the torrential rainy season. I was also not aware that most of the houses were not insulated. The combination of coldness and humidity in winter made me feel colder than I ever was in Manitoba. There is nothing like climbing between damp, cold sheets to engender a cozy night's sleep. In spite of that, Vancouver is a beautiful city with magnificent periods of sunshine and exquisite beaches.

I was a bit naïve about dangers in a big city. One night, not all that late but dark, I was walking home by the most direct route. It was somewhere along Hastings and Pender, I think. It was what might be described as a disreputable area. As I walked along, I observed a group of about seven individuals who definitely deserved the same description as the neighborhood.

They totally blocked the sidewalk, leaving me with two sensible alternatives. One would be to walk out into the street around them and the other was to turn around and scurry back the way I had come. I chose 'none of the above'. I didn't like the idea of turning my back on them nor did I like going out of my way to get around them. I just kept walking straight ahead, deviating only enough to avoid walking straight into any one of them.

With a firm but pleasant voice I said, "Excuse me, please."

I didn't avoid looking at them, but I avoided eye contact. I had read somewhere that you should never make eye contact with angry dogs or wild animals. They didn't exactly fit into either category, but I figured the idea was about the same. Individuals moved just enough to let me pass without physical contact, but they were well inside my usual personal space allocation.

I wasn't worried until they were behind me. Although I felt very vulnerable, I kept walking at my normal pace. All went well. A few days later I read about a person who had been put into the hospital by a gang in that same area. I think they let me pass because they figured no one could be that stupid unless there were police all around the area and I was the decoy for their sting operation.

My educational experience at UBC started well. Most of the classes were alright except for being rather old fashioned and/or weird. There was a class on discipline that involved such things as how to strap a student without accidentally causing bruising (hold him by the wrist to protect it) and how to avoid hitting yourself on the leg if the student were to pull his hand away. I was taking the classes for teaching high school Math and Science. In the Science methods course we spent weeks on how to construct a diorama of an Eskimo village. It was a skill I have never called upon to use since. Needless to say, I was getting good marks and putting in the time. For the first time in my life I was attending classes regularly because attendance was rigidly enforced, at all times, and with dire consequences for absenteeism.

For my first session of practice teaching I was assigned to one of the largest high schools in the area. There were over 100 teachers and over 2000 students. It was a very different environment from any schools I had been in previously. My assignment was to teach Grade 9 Mathematics to an assembly line of students. I would teach the same lesson six times a day as students filed in and out of the room. Then the next day it would be the next lesson six times as the students march like robots through the course. It was not what I would have wanted. It was boring and a useless learning experience for me, but so-be-it I thought. I never learned a single student's name or face. I felt I had done well to learn the names of a few of the teachers.

Then some more courses and a different diorama followed by my next student teaching assignment Grade 4 Art, Language Arts, and another subject. Surprising, but at least I had the same students more than once a day and could work with them in their process of learning. I was looking forward to a real teaching experience. Within a couple of days I learned that one of the students in our Education program had been assigned to student teach Grade 12 Physics. She was immediately reduced to tears because she had never even taken Physics in school and was planning to teach primary grades when she graduated. She had approached the Dean of Education but he had turned a deaf ear. To me, the solution was obvious—she should switch assignments with me.

My initial meeting with the Dean was short but not sweet.

He said, "NO," with the explanation that it was done deliberately so that students would practice teach a level and subject as far as possible from what they planned to teach after they graduated.

My reaction, loosely translated, was something like, "Huh?"

He explained further. It would be an experience they would never get otherwise. Students would have their whole career to practice their subject and grade of choice. I must admit that he was right . . . up to a point. For me it was a good experience working with primary grades, and one I did use many years later when I was employed as consultant/supervisor/coordinator for all grades in the Portage School Division.

I must have seemed unconvinced because he added a gem of wisdom for the girl who couldn't manage to learn two years of Physics overnight to keep ahead of her students.

"You don't need to know the subject. You just have to know how to teach," he said.

My response was, "I'd like to see you try to teach an advanced course in Greek without ever having taken Greek."

Our discussion rapidly went downhill from there and I was verbally thrown out of his office with language inappropriate for a Dean. I tried to reason with him on a couple of other occasions until he refused to see me.

I wrote him a letter trying to explain the situation from my perspective including a reminder that I had a year of teaching experience.

He wrote back to me, including the statement, "Whatever teaching ability you might have had you obviously left in Manitoba."

It was a letter I kept as a memento . . . or as ammunition just in case there were future repercussions . . . and there were.

It seemed prudent for me to back off at this point. A few days later the student teacher dropped out of the Education program. I was sad because I thought she could have become a good teacher. I didn't follow my inclination to have one last meeting with the Dean. It would have made me feel so much better, but it was too late to help her.

The rest of the year went as well as could be expected and I was finishing with A's and B's. Three weeks before the graduation ceremonies, the Dean announced that in order to make teaching more of a profession like Engineering (he actually said that) there would be an additional four week session of practice teaching starting right after graduation so it could be worked in before the public schools closed for the year.

This was a problem for me because I had by then accepted a lucrative summer job in the research department of the Flin Flon zinc mine. I took a deep breath and tried to see the Dean. Over the intercom he told his secretary to tell me he would not see me. I asked her if he was alone or if he had someone in his office. She said he was alone. She should have lied to me. I went to his door, knocked firmly, walked in and told him it was his job to see students and I was a student. As you might guess, we did not have an amicable discussion about the possibility of my taking the final session in the fall because I needed to go to my summer job. He was not prepared to be flexible; it was now or never. I thanked him, sarcastically, and left for my job in Flin Flon.

***

~ It Pays To Check ~

After I had left UBC I decided to check my transcript. They were not sent out to students, only to other people, so I got a copy sent to a friend in order to see it. It itemized my course work (all passing grades) and noted my Practice Teaching as incomplete.

So far, so good. Then at the bottom of the transcript there was a typed notation: 'FAILED YEAR - NO CREDIT'.

I thought this to be a bit harsh, so I sent a polite letter to the university president outlining my experiences with the Dean of Education, including a copy of his rude letter to me.

A couple of months later I again checked a copy of my official university transcript. It came with the typed notation at the bottom deleted by being covered with 'white out'.

A bit tacky, but efficient.

Flin Flon, Manitoba

Notice the "above rock" sewer line

Mining In Flin Flon

Flin Flon is a northern mining town. The city's website calls it 'a city built on the rocks,' and it really is. Sewer lines run above ground (or more correctly, 'above rock') and are boxed in so the top of the box can serve as a sidewalk. People used dynamite to landscape their front yards.

The mine buildings straddle the border between Manitoba and Saskatchewan with the boundary line painted across the floor in bright yellow. When you were hired, instructions were given by the union as to which side of the line you should crawl to in case of an accident in order to get the better compensation benefits.

When I got to Flin Flon, I was temporarily assigned to mucking underground. Mucking consists of shoveling the loose, often wet, rock material back into an ore car to keep the track clear. It is not an intellectually challenging job. A bus took us from the parking area to the main shaft which went straight down into the earth for a distance of somewhere between half a mile and a mile, depending on what level you were working. There are roadways (called 'levels') running out from the elevator. Blasting the rock with dynamite and removing the rock containing zinc and traces of other valuable ores create these horizontal levels, and railway tracks are constructed along them.

New roadways are created at lower levels or in different directions when the vein of ore gets too small to be economically useful. Trains of ore cars run back and forth along the levels carrying the ore back to the elevator. At intervals a large hole (called a 'winze') went from one level to the one below, like a bottomless hopper. This allowed ore and supplies to be loaded into an ore car by dropping it through the winze from the level above.

Working underground was an experience I will never forget. Imagine this. You step onto a platform enclosed by vertical metal bars, hanging from a thick steel cable. As the miners step into the cage it wobbles from side to side and bounces up-and-down enough to make you doubt the wisdom of trusting your safety to it. When the elevator stops at the level on which you will be working, the long cable stretches enough that the elevator rises and falls enough to scare the wits out of you.

When you get off the elevator you walk along a railway track through a long tunnel just big enough for the train of ore cars to pass through with maybe an inch or two of clearance between the side of the ore car and either wall of the roadway. Every twenty-five yards or so there is a widened section of the roadway wall just big enough to accommodate four people in safety as the train rumbled by. Then you would continue on your trek to the work site until the next train came along.

On my first expedition underground there were three of us who were going to muck in the same area.

As we walked along the train track, one of them pointed out a widened space and explained, "If there is a train coming get in one of those."

I thought a bit more explanation might be in order, but that was all I was getting. Conversation was not high on the priority list of underground activities. Maybe it comes from having your vision narrowly focused by the little helmet light shining into the darkness.

The three of us were walking along the track when I heard the ominous rumble of a train. Panic. Where is the closest passing bay? Is it better to run toward the train or away from it? And from which way is the train coming? The reverberation of the noise, and my confusion, made it difficult for me to know. There was no time to try solving it like one of those train travel problems so ubiquitous in high school algebra classes. And certainly it was no time to get caught in the donkey between two bales of hay dilemma.

Fortunately, one of my buddies (anyone is a friend at a time like this) sensed my concern and nodded his head to indicate we should go forward. I must have set a new mine speed record as I raced down the track and threw myself into the passing bay. I looked back and saw the other two experienced miners laughing at me as they ambled along and arrived at the passing bay just seconds before the train. They stepped to safety just as it sped past us. It was my first lesson in dealing with the closeness of immediate death in the mines. I rationalized it by thinking about how, in a big city, we will stand on a sidewalk as a city bus roars by. The first time it is scary and you stand three feet back. Then, over time, you become desensitized to the danger, ignore it, and stand just inches away from the bus as it roars past.

You have probably heard of the big psychological question, "Does a person run because he is scared, or is he scared because he runs?"

I had no reason to be scared by this situation. If I stayed with the experienced pair, I knew I would be safe because they knew what they were doing. I ran only because I thought I should be on the safe side. When I arrived at the passing bay I was really scared. Interesting. Thinking back to running from the barking dogs when we were stealing a turkey, I think the running came first (as a way to escape). The fear I felt when I arrived at the safety of the car was a product of the running, probably brought on by the increased adrenaline in my blood stream.

During the time I worked there, there were several times when collections were taken on the bus ride back from the mine to help the family of a worker who had died. One person stepped onto the elevator when it wasn't there. No parts of his body arrived at the bottom of the shaft. Another time a person was repairing the track behind closed fire doors in spite of it being a violation of the safety rules. The train slammed into the closed doors, slapped them open, and crushed the miner against the roadway wall. This was also a violation of the safety rules because the driver should have stopped the train in front of the doors and opened them manually. But that would have taken time, and the pay was calculated on the amount of ore delivered. Drivers rarely stopped the train for closed doors.

Even with the constant reminders of the dangerous environment, experienced miners took unnecessary chances. Dynamite for blasting was shipped in wooden containers, which took time to open. The fastest way to open a box was to have it delivered to one level above where it would be used and then drop it down through the winze to the lower level. The impact was just right to break open the box and spill out the dynamite ready for use—unless it happened to trigger an explosion at the same time. Then you would need to have another box delivered.

Do you remember the Road Runner cartoon in which Wylie Coyote stands under a big pile of lodged rocks and pokes at them with a pole until they come free and fall onto him? Occasionally, the rocks being dropped into the ore car on a lower level would jam the winze. What faster way is there to loosen them than to stand under the ton of rock, poke it with a pole until it loosens, and hope you can get out of the way in time? Usually there was plenty of time to get out of the way but sometimes not quite enough.

I was ecstatic when I was transferred to work in the research department of the zinc smelter plant. It was above ground level and had access to fresh air and sunlight. And there were no sounds of dynamite blasting on a level above or the rumbling of trainloads of ore. In short, it was boring. Delightfully boring. To my surprise, I discovered Jack was working in another area of the smelter for the summer. I did say we didn't communicate much, didn't I? We had been working in the same area of the mine for over a week and I hadn't known where he was working.

Jack and I spent some recreational time together. I lived in the city; he lived on an island and swam about forty-five minutes across the lake to and from work. I didn't even know he could swim. I was very impressed and wondered what else he had hidden behind his shy chuckles. He hadn't completed a credit in Grade 12 Literature, so I helped him study the novel by showing him how to answer exam-type questions. He said he would show me how to party on his little island if I would buy the beer for him and his underage friends. I didn't think of it as breaking the law, just more as being a few years ahead of my time (actually, 13 years) in realizing that the age of majority should be lowered. In Manitoba the drinking age was lowered from 21 to 18 years in 1970. I didn't think there was much chance they could get in trouble with the law since the party was on Jack's island in the middle of a lake.

I had read somewhere that in North America people mature one year earlier every decade. When I was in Grade 12 the students decided to have a beard-growing contest with the teachers. It was a disaster for the students. The best we could do was to produce a few scattered tufts of facial hair. I managed two pretty obvious tufts of red hair on each corner of my chin. Being red, made it look even less impressive compared to one of our teachers who could grow a full, heavy, black, beard on a couple of week's notice. That was in 1950 and it is now 2000. At a rate of one year earlier per decade, that would mean that students should mature five years earlier now, and students now in Grade 7 should be able to grow a beard as good as mine was in Grade 12. It comes out pretty close. When I look at Grade 8 students now they are about the same maturity level as I was in Grade 12. Obviously, this relationship can't be a straight-line one. The rate of early maturity has to slow down with the passage of time, probably asymptotic at some point.

There were three of us employed in the research department. Two were regular staff and I was the summer help. The mine hired university students in hopes they would eventually be interested in a permanent job—not to actually do anything useful. Our job was to take samples from the various stages of the ore as it was processed from solid form into liquid suitable for the zinc to be electroplated out onto large cathode plates. It was an easy job but very important in making sure the whole system would work smoothly. One day we found the plating solution to be unusually acidic. We reported it to the smelter boss and were told keep a watch on it. So we did frequent checks and found the situation getting progressively worse. We went as a group and reported our findings, recommending he shut down the system until it was corrected because it could make the zinc very difficult to strip off the cathode plates.

His reaction was, "I've been working here for ten years and we've never had trouble with the zinc sticking."

We went back to our regular job of sitting and waiting.

By the end of the day he came to us and asked, "Do you have any ideas how to get solidly plated zinc off the cathodes?"

"You will be lucky if you can get it off with a hammer and chisel. Electroplating is supposed to be permanent," was our unsympathetic response.

It did provide a week of fulltime employment for a dozen hammer-and-chisel experts.

There were good things about Flin Flon. One was the lovers' lane provided by the slag pits. The downside was there weren't many eligible girls. It may not sound romantic, but the molten hot slag cooling slowly provided a magnificent glow of simmering light in the sky.

Another amusement was the summer swim to the block of ice left in the middle of the lake as it slowly melted in the spring. Maybe it wasn't as great as we thought, but it was all we had. However, there was great fishing. Lake trout was large, plentiful and easy to catch if you had the right equipment. They lived deep in the lake and that required more equipment than I was prepared to acquire. I never did catch one, but I did catch lots of pickerel in the spring while the water was still cold. In the early spring when the lakes flooded the ditches, a person could stop anywhere by the side of the road and catch dinner out of a ditch. Flin Flon was full of unusual experiences.

Life As A Meteorologist

When my job at Flin Flon ended, I drove back to Vancouver in my trusty Morris Minor convertible. It was a knee-jerk reaction. I hadn't completed my last practice teaching session so I just automatically went back to Vancouver without thinking about it.

When I got there, I realized I didn't want to finish my Faculty of Education. I remembered what it had been like and if that represented what teaching was all about, I wanted no part of it. So, I went to the 'jobs available' bulletin board and found an interesting job in Toronto for the university's meteorology program. I fired off my application and, after I had mailed it, noticed the position opened at the beginning of January. And here it was September, so I could have a bit of a holiday. That would be nice.

Al needed a car to elope (in a hurry) so I sold him my Morris Minor at a fair market value (one dollar). It had just traveled from Flin Flon and all it asked was a new tire. It was a good car in that we never even had to consider that it might not be up to the lengthy trip back to Winnipeg. I've had expensive new cars since then that required a lot more checking over before daring to venture on a trip of that magnitude. I bought an old Plymouth coupe for a few hundred dollars and drove it around in Vancouver. My friends said—publicly and loudly—that I was an accident going somewhere to happen because I kept forgetting the Plymouth was three times the size of the Morris and didn't handle well. It generally felt like it was traveling twice as fast as it actually was, and this made for a scary ride. After a couple of weeks, I began to feel lost. My friends were all doing something useful and I was doing nothing except spending the hard-earned money I had saved. That is just an expression. After I got out of the underground work, which was hard, sweaty work, I didn't do more than 2 hours a day of anything that required me to be more than half awake.

Then I got an inspiration. I might as well be heading to Toronto for my new job. It never occurred to me that I might not get the job. As far as I was concerned, I had applied, was qualified, and so of course I would get the job. I packed my oversized metal suitcase, which had been traveling around the country with me for a few years now, and my trusty euphonium in its traveling case and headed for Toronto via the United States. I had always traveled at full throttle in the Morris, so I automatically did the same in the Plymouth until the motor dissolved in clouds of steam, hot oil and atrociously nasty metal noises. The Morris would never have behaved in such a rude manner. I sold the car for parts and hopped on a Greyhound bus to finish the trip.

When I arrived in Toronto I initially stayed with a relative until I found a place of my own. It was a half-hour subway ride (45 minutes in rush hour) from the Meteorological Offices at the university, but I appreciated having a place to stay. I ventured downtown and enquired as to the progress of my application. When I told the fellow in charge I was there from Vancouver and had nothing to do with my life until my job started, he suggested that they could use an assistant for some research they were doing and I might like to do that. It was an easy job, organizing weather data, and doing some office work. The pay was good so I agreed and started the next morning.

Although the subway was fast and efficient, it was still a big waste of time. I found a nice little rooming place with meals very near the Meteorological Office. It was operated by a formal Chinese couple who ran it like a restaurant except without any menu or choices. It was spotlessly clean, antiseptic and the meals repetitious. There would be a bowl of soup with one cellophane wrapped soda cracker. Condiments were all in small, individual sealed containers. There were no extras or flexibility. There were four other people staying there, but they appeared only at mealtime (as I guess I did, too) and conversation with the meal seemed to be an intrusion. I stayed only a couple of weeks before searching out a different place.

I found a place in a German section of the city. It was near where I was happily working and the people seemed nice. They spoke no English and I spoke little German, but even so we had more conversation than in my previous place. There was lots of variety in the food and it was always well prepared with typical German enthusiasm. I thought I had found the ideal place until one dinner when we had ribs with sauerkraut. The ribs were small and thin, but bigger than rabbit. I had eaten rabbit stew on the farm, and I knew they weren't rabbit. I had eaten sheep, but they were smaller and thinner than the sheep I had eaten. We did some of our usual informal sign language discussion and eliminated a lot of things they might have been. The ribs were delicious, but somehow I couldn't bring myself to do more than taste them, knowing what they weren't, and suspecting what they were.

My new job presented me with one big problem. It would be another month before I would get a pay cheque. My summer savings, such as they had been, were fast running out. I bid *auf Wiedersehen* to my German friends, and got a tiny, cheap room close to the university with no meals. The last couple of weeks before I got my first pay cheque I was living on peanut butter and bread. I couldn't even afford a bottle of coke. Toward the end of the month I was finding bread to be a luxury. That's how broke I was.

I was just doing miscellaneous jobs until my real job started in January, so I was available when they suddenly needed a relief person for the International Geophysical Year (1957–58) project on measuring the thickness of the upper air ozone layer. The equipment was set up at Moosonee, north of Toronto, on the tip of James Bay, which is available only by train from Toronto. The person who was operating it was suffering from the isolation and was badly in need of some R&R. I was a good fit for the job because of my Physics and Math background and I was ready and willing to go on moment's notice.

My pay would be the same as in Toronto, but with a northern allowance, isolation bonus, and included room and board. My cheques were deposited directly into a Toronto bank because I had no need for money. The only commercial venture in Moosonee was a Hudson Bay trading post for the half dozen local residents and the Eskimo/ Aboriginal people living within dog sled range. The 'store' was full of tied and stacked bales of hides, which were used by the residents for any purchases more expensive than a candy bar. I really felt like a one of the early explorers. Anything the store didn't stock—which was pretty well everything—had to be ordered from the town of Kapuskasing and shipped in by train. I quickly learned things about ordering liquor; order twice as much as you wanted because half of it would mysteriously disappear on the train trip, and have them pack it well or the rest of it would get broken. Kapuskasing had a bakery that specialized in the insertion of a bottle of whisky into a fresh loaf of bread for shipment.

I learned why there was an isolation bonus. From the observation tower, which was used for taking weather observations, I took photos in all four compass directions to send home. They showed nothing but ice and snow as far as the eye could see—no trees, no nothing. However, listening to the Northern Lights was a surprising experience because scientifically, they cannot produce sound (oh, yes, and scientifically, a bumblebee can't fly, either). Also called the *aurora borealis*, they occur at an altitude of over 100 kilometers, which is almost a vacuum, and hence (scientifically) cannot transmit sound to the earth. They are visible in most of Canada as streaks of moving colors in the northern sky. In Moosonee, they regularly filled the sky with shimmering sheets of changing colors accompanied by crackling sounds as if the entire sky were having a short-circuit. Maybe the Northern Lights weren't making the sounds, but something certainly was, and they seemed to be the most likely cause. Or maybe, whatever causes the light display also causes other electro-magnetic disturbances closer to ground level which we can hear but don't see. Either way, it was delightfully impressive.

I was back into sharing my sleeping quarters with a roommate. It was a hulking, overweight, shiny white chunk of metal sitting in the center of the room and spreading out to occupy most of the room. Its sole purpose was to encase a rectangular prism the size of a single section of a Kit Kat chocolate bar, hold it *very* steady and allow the light to be dispersed onto a soot blackened disc. Its name was, 'Dobson Ozone Spectrophotometer'. We called it, 'it', for short. At least, it was quiet and well behaved, although rather demanding. I slept on a cot huddled on one side of the room near the heater.

There was a predawn reading to be taken before sunrise if the sky was clear. So as a minimum, I had to wake up two hours before dawn to cast a bleary eye skywards to see if I needed to make the dreaded 'Umkehr' reading. If it was cloudy I could go back to sleep. Sometimes the clouds I saw may have been more in my eye than in the sky. Isn't there a saying something like, 'clouds are in the eye of the beholder'?

There was enough to do to keep busy: calibrate the machine, take hourly readings, use a candle to coat the reading disks evenly with a layer of carbon soot, record the information on the carbon disks, and sleep. Also, there were weather observations to take twice a day and send to Toronto for compiling weather maps. I assisted in releasing balloons with equipment to record barometric pressure and temperature, and recording cloud types, size and height. I also used alcohol to polished the glass domes containing radiation sensors and discovered how cold alcohol is on a bare hand when the temperature is approaching minus forty.

It was in recording cloud heights that I discovered I was deficient in depth perception. The person with whom I worked could just look up and say how high the cloud was. No matter how I tried, I couldn't guess the height of a cloud. I had known that I couldn't estimate the distance of any object from me unless I had some other objects to use as reference points, such as telephone poles on a highway. It had just never occurred to me that most people could just look at an object and estimate its distance. I later learned it has to do with the brain interpreting muscle tension of the eyes as distance when they focus on an object.

It was weird having no use for money. A few of the people (including the local RCMP officer) played poker using paper chits in place of money to make atrociously high bets. When the officer was rotated back to civilization (possibly owing tens of thousands of dollars) it was assumed the chits were null and void. I didn't play poker at the best of times and I wasn't going to start losing money to a police officer on the assumption he understood it was only play-money.

When I returned to Toronto, I had more money in my bank account than it had ever had before at one time. And by then, I was getting a regular monthly cheque so I felt free to spend it foolishly, which I did for a couple of weeks until financial sanity set in, which it did, thanks to my Scottish heritage. We had a picture of one of my grandfathers, with his piecing eyes, clenched jaw and muttonchop sideburns staring down at us from a wall in our living room at home on the farm. I can still see him clearly in my mind whenever I get reckless with my money.

Living for a month without needing money had made it lose all sense of value to me. Looking back at my bankbook later I saw regular hundred dollar withdrawals every day—and that was in 1958 dollars—until I had my bank balance back to its usual manageable amount. The only significant purchase I made at that time was to buy another Morris Minor Convertible.

I also worked for several weeks at the Air Force base in Trenton, Ontario as meteorologist. We were given an honorary rank (Flight Lieutenant, I think) so that our statements about flying conditions could be taken as a significant order. It also entitled us to eat in the Officers' Mess and enjoy Friday lobster feasts with all the trimmings, including exotic liquids. No matter how much I tried to count stripes and bars I could never figure out the assorted ranks and who outranked whom. I became an equal opportunity saluter. I saluted anyone in uniform. I got a few confused looks, and a lot of smiles, but generally people just returned the salute.

One aspect of our training was to become familiar with the up and down drafts in the atmosphere. A group of us went up in a big cargo plane that was deliberately flown through thunderclouds during a storm. It was unnerving to observe the plane's wings flapping as it alternated between falling and rising air currents. They did assure us that the lightning flashing around us was harmless. It did help me to remember that in a hollow metal container the charge is on the outside, and we were on the inside. Who says knowledge of Physics isn't useful?

Back at the university, while learning how to draw weather maps, I came to the realization that anyone, or even an exceptionally bright monkey, could do this as well or better than I could. This revelation occurred in August, just as everyone was gearing up for the opening of public school classes and purchasing school supplies. I resigned from the program, packed my metal suitcase and euphonium, sold my

Morris Minor to my current roommate ($1), and hopped a Greyhound Bus back to Winnipeg.

I had a bank balance over $1000. As usual, I was at a crossroad in my life. The Mexican peso was low compared to the Canadian dollar. A bit of mental arithmetic convinced me I could live in Mexico for a year on the money I had in the bank if I lived on the beach. I knew nothing else about Mexico, but it was all very appealing and romantic.

I knew I liked teaching, but it wasn't as easy as living on a beach in Mexico drinking Tequila. At that time I had never tasted Tequila, but the name had a nice ring to it and it got good press in movies. If I knew then what I know now about Tequila I probably wouldn't have been considering Mexico.

Be that as it may, I spent a day and a night wandering up and down Portage Avenue trying to make a decision between teaching and Mexico. It was that donkey with the two bales of hay situation again. I was never any good with choices, so I did the only mature thing under the circumstances. I flipped a coin. Teaching won.

It was now only a week before school was scheduled to open. There were very few schools that did not have their staff in place, and there was usually some good reason for that.

Dobson Spectrophotometer
http://ozone.gi.alaska.edu/dobson.htm

Northern Lights over the tree line

Cranberry Portage

The bus ride from Winnipeg took me through Swan River on the way to Cranberry Portage, which is a small settlement half way between The Pas and Flin Flon. The town had a hotel that sold beer, but few other recreational activities, except for curling. The surrounding area provided an abundance of lake-related activities. I was back to living without hot or cold running water and bathing in a metal washtub using a sponge. At least there was a diesel-operated electric generator for lights and other limited electrical uses.

I did some boating and fishing—mostly just holding a fishing rod so it would look like I was doing something—but not curling. Midwinter, I found out that a few of the school students were on a curling team that was highly regarded by the community. There was no one interested in arranging for them to go to Winnipeg for a bonspiel, possibly because it was a 10-hour drive to Winnipeg and this being 1959, it was considered to be quite an expedition. Up to this time, I had never even watched a curling game nor touched a curling rock. Who better than me to chaperone and coach them?

I arranged to borrow a car, reserved two rooms in a downtown hotel, so we would be able to get the big-city feel within walking distance, and looked after the entry details. When we arrived in Winnipeg, I discovered that bonspiels start very early in the morning. Why did nobody think to tell me that? I was counting on having a nice holiday, but found I had to get up early in order to drive the team around the city to the various rinks. They won a couple of games, but were clearly outclassed. It was a good experience for them anyway, and even some fun for me.

A few years later, when I was teaching in Portage la Prairie, one of the teams was short one member. Emboldened by my experience in

Cranberry Portage, I volunteered. It was the first time I had touched a curling rock, but as lead there seemed to be only two things I needed to be able to do: either aim at the broom and try to make the rock stop where the skip indicated, or aim at a rock belonging to the opposing team and knock it out. Big deal. We won a cup (it was in the consolation round). My wife, Wilma was not pleased because she was from a curling family and had curled for years, but I was the only one in the family to win a trophy. Of course, I never curled again. Why should I? I had my trophy.

I was employed as principal for the Grade 1–11 school and teacher for Grades 9, 10 and 11, with all three grades in one room at the same time. I also 'taught' Grade 7 and 8 French, mostly as a way of having contact with these students who were in a different building about 100 yards away on the other side of town. I had a fair reading and writing knowledge of French and with the assistance of tapes managed to provide an appropriate spoken French experience. The students enjoyed it and, although they maybe didn't learn much French, it wasn't harmful for them.

The Grade 4 teacher did not like Art and so I took his class in exchange for his doing Physical Education with my class. I knew nothing about teaching Art so I improvised by reading them descriptive literature or poetry and had them draw or paint the imagery.

As principal, I had to fill out monthly attendance reports for all the grades and numerous other departmental forms designed to keep full-time principals busy. My courses in the Faculty of Education had not provided me with any information about being a principal, so the first month I just pretended I knew what I was doing and filled the forms out as I saw fit.

After a pointed letter from the Department of Education asking me what I thought I was doing, and a phone call from me to them explaining that I didn't have a clue, everything went along smoothly on that front. They were very understanding and helpful, and I soon learned the shortcuts.

Keep in mind I had only really taught that one year of High School in Swan River and that was to a class of twenty-some students all of them taking the same grade and subject together. Here I was expected to teach three grade levels all in the same room at the same time. Granted, it was only eleven students, but how does one teach three different lessons at the same time? It's very simple. You don't. By the end of my year at Swan River I had begun to realize that the less I taught, the more the students learned. It became crystal clear in Cranberry Portage that my role was to organize work activities for the three grades. I could teach a short lesson to one-third of the class while the other two-thirds worked. Most of my time was spent working individually with the students interspersed with five-minute mini lessons.

While I was at Cranberry Portage, the School Division completed a new modern school building—with running water! We moved into the new building midyear. Most of the younger students had never seen water flow out of a tap. The flushing process of a modern toilet was fascinating to them. They could watch the sight of swirling water for hours at a time. For the first couple of days, checking the washrooms I would frequently find all the stalls being used by elementary grade students continually flushing the toilet and staring mesmerized by the continuous swirl of disappearing water. At our regular student assembly I explained the situation and pointed out that if water rationing were required it would be very inconvenient for everyone. Most of then understood and helped monitor the use by the ones who didn't.

The new building had one long, shiny, slippery hallway. It cried out to be raced on . . . and it was. There did not seem to be any logical reason not to allow races (except that the elementary grade teachers didn't approve of racing on principle) so the students and I made a compromise. Races would be held only at authorized times. I considered it to be part of the Physical Education program of the school.

It was fortunate I had the experience of High School at Swan River so I knew what was necessary to prepare the Grade 10 and 11 students for the departmental exams that determined their passing or failing. I had gone to high school in Saskatchewan in a school that gave exemptions from final exams for students with good grades, so I had never written a Departmental Exam. The Faculty of Education at UBC had deliberately given me no instruction or practical experience with my chosen field of high school. The Dean of Education must have been right again because things did work out for me . . . eventually and with a lot of work.

My landlady was a motherly lady and always helpful. She would nag me about writing home and one time when I balked, she dictated a letter to my mother for me to send. My mother always said it was the best letter I had ever written. My landlady reminded me to leave my door open if I had a visitor, and was disappointed that such a nice boy as I would drive a 'show off' car like the Triumph.

She also introduced me to a delicacy of the area—pickerel livers. They were a delicacy because they were good only in the spring when the water was icy cold, and were scarce because it was a lot of extra work to obtain because they are very small. They were similar to mild chicken liver but tastier. I had never had them before or since.

The Manitoba Teachers' Society (MTS) in Flin Flon and I collaborated in setting up a local branch in Cranberry Portage. This was my introduction to a professional organization, but for me, it was more of a social gathering as far as I was concerned.

It was a good year with nice people, but I missed the level of civilization offered by big cities. I did not like living in a really big city like Toronto or Vancouver. They were too big for me. At one time, I had a girlfriend across the city and it was a two-hour drive there and back for a three-hour date. I did like the cultural activities only a big city can offer, so I decided I should live in a small city reasonable close to a biggish city like Winnipeg. I studied maps in my spare time and decided on a small city, Portage la Prairie (usually just called 'Portage'), about an hour drive from Winnipeg. As luck would have it, they were advertising for a high school science teacher. I was hired by mail, subject to an interview during the summer. It was a fortuitous decision and one that led to my 35 years working in the Portage School Division in a variety of roles.

I also met my future wife while we were both teaching at the Portage Collegiate.

***

~ Diligence Is Important ~

Primary grade teacher (accosting me on the playground with a burnt paper match clutched accusingly between finger and thumb): "I found this right over there. What should we do about it?"

Me (taking it from her gingerly between thumb and finger): "Thank you. I'll look after it."

I was diligent after that to tour around the area before school every day to pick up any droppings from the real world. Problem solved.

***

~ Inspector Reports - The Wrong Way ~

Up until 1985, The Department of Education employed school inspectors whose job it was to inspect the educational program in every school, including the teachers. They arrived twice a year and would spend an hour in each classroom.

I was teaching in Cranberry Portage in a classroom with Grades 9–11 all at the same time. I met with my inspector prior to his visit.

"I want to see you teach a full length class," he suggested.

"But I never teach for more than ten minutes at a time," I countered.

"I want to see you teach an hour lesson."

"But what about the other two grades? What are they supposed to be doing while I am teaching a lesson to one grade?"

"I want to see a full lesson."

"Wouldn't you rather see what I usually do on an average day?"

"I want to see an hour lesson," he announced as he left.

He saw me teach the class several five-minute lessons, as I always did. I got a really bad report.

***

~ Inspector Reports ~ The Right Way ~

A couple of years later, when I was teaching in Portage, one of the staff members told me the Inspector liked to see things posted around the room.

I taught in the Physics lab because we were short of actual classrooms, and there wasn't much actual wall space. Most of the walls were cupboards or windows. I covered every vertical surface with charts, diagrams, and student work without any regard to relevance or logic. I even put them over all the windows. It was inconvenient that I couldn't open any of the cupboards without taking down some display and I ended up with lab equipment piled on the floor.

"Uh, don't you think you're overdoing it?" the vice-principal asked me apprehensively.

I looked around, laughed inwardly, and said, "It looks alright to me."

The inspector came in, said hello and started scrutinizing my wall displays. He went slowly and methodically all around the room, ignoring the students and me. I tried to talk to him but he would have none of that. He spent his whole hour studying my displays and left without comment.

I received an excellent report from him on my teaching skills.

*** *

~ Gardening In Manitoba ~

I was planting seeds in my new Manitoba garden with 'help' from my new mother-in-law. I noticed she was going along behind me, picking half the seeds out of the row as I was seeding.

Me: "Why are you taking the seeds out?"

Frances: "This is Manitoba. All the seeds will germinate here."

Me: "Oh, right. I'm used to Saskatchewan where most of the seeds never germinate because it is so dry. And half of the new plants are eaten by the grasshoppers."

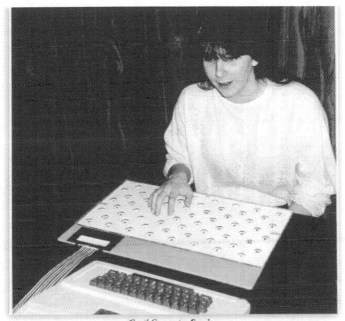

Cacti Computer Services
Pressure Sensitive Keyboard

Static Electricity - van de Graaf generator
photo courtesy of the American Museum of Science and Energy, Oak Ridge, TN

Thirty-Five Years Teaching In Portage

I had driven through the city of Portage a dozen times through the years because it is a city on the Trans-Canada highway, just before or after Winnipeg depending on whether you are traveling east or west across Canada. It was not memorable—just a possible break on a long boring drive. As I have mentioned before, I chose this location, from the distant perspective of northern Manitoba, because it was only an hour drive from Winnipeg. I had absolutely no first hand knowledge of the city or its school system. For me, those were irrelevant details. My interest was in Winnipeg as being big enough, but not too big. Portage was going to be a nice, quiet place to live, and maybe work, while I commuted to and from Winnipeg for my real life.

Here I was, applying for a job as a high school teacher at the Portage Collegiate Institute (PCI). That's what they had decided to name it when the building was constructed in 1896 . . . an 'institute'. In 1994, PCI celebrated its one-hundredth birthday. That would actually be its 98th birthday, but the organizers either weren't very good at arithmetic or were too impatient to wait for two more years to have a party. A lot of people behave strangely when they are being kept away from a party. Besides, I suppose a little dissemblance never hurt anyone, and it does seem to be totally acceptable in war, business and politics.

The school had about 600 students in Grades 9 to 12, with twenty-one teachers when I started there. Its student population increased steadily year by year for a few years to a maximum of about 1000 without increasing the physical size of the building. The halls were crowded during class changes. There was a strictly enforced 'keep to the right, and keep moving' rule.

As might be expected, I was assigned the less academically inclined students and Grade 9 Science—not a high prestige course. It took me until Christmas to catch onto this, but it wouldn't have made any difference anyway. I was low man on the totem pole. At least, I was teaching in a real school as a qualified teacher for the first time and I was coming in with some really good skills from my experiences in Swan River and Cranberry Portage. I had a good year and it was the beginning of a satisfying thirty-five year run. At last, I had found where I had been going all these years (although I have had a few misgivings over the years at PCI when I wasn't sure what it was that I wanted to do when I grew up).

The high school program (Grades 9 –12) was organized with homogeneous grouping (students of equal academic ability grouped together in the same class). The classes were identified alphabetically from highest ability to the lowest. My homeroom was Room 9-I (the lowest grade in the school and the students with the lowest academic abilities). I totally loved the kids. They were open, honest and generally outgoing. So maybe they weren't the best students, but that was why I was there—to teach them. It was a challenge but they responded well to demonstrations, real-life examples, experiments, games and general fooling around. Starting with my second year I moved more into teaching Grade 11 and 12 Chemistry, Physics and Mathematics. However, I continued to have the lower academic ability classes (as in, 11-H) as my 'homeroom' class, usually held in the Physics lab, and I wouldn't have wanted it any other way. I enjoyed the less academically inclined students and they enjoyed it that I would try out my Physics demonstrations on them before school started. Often, I put a contrived 'magic' aspect to them. The van de Graaf generator was a useful tool for studying properties of static electricity, but mostly was just for the fun for making hair stand on end on a student's arms and head.

Errol and I started a school Science Club in my second year there. I enjoyed the less formal environment and the range of ages in the clubs. It was fun working with students in this way. I gradually started a variety of other clubs, including Chess, Touchdown Quiz and Reach For the Top. All I needed was four or more students with a common interest and I'd set up a club for it.

I found a room to rent upstairs in a house with two other people my age and within walking distance of PCI. My Triumph was a 'chick magnet' for eligible young teachers throughout the summer and late fall and I enjoyed taking dates to Winnipeg. Some of them, especially Shirley, loved the experience of going 100 mph (160 km/hr) for short periods of time on the way to and from Winnipeg. This was to be my first winter with my ragtop Triumph. I soon discovered that although England made excellent automobiles it did not have a clue how to make a heater for one. In fact, the heater, bought as an optional accessory, was almost useless. My trips to Winnipeg in the winter with a date were a wonder to behold. I had to drive with an ice scraper in one hand just to maintain a few inches of ice-free windshield to peer through. Winter boots and gloves were essential. As you might guess, for their second date most of them were happy to spend the time in Portage—a significant financial saving for me.

My first year at PCI was relatively uneventful. I think I must have had the help of a guardian angel to dodge most of the 'rookie mistake' bullets, because it certainly wasn't due to any caution on my part. My car attracted lots of student attention and I enjoyed the unexpected popularity generated from giving them rides and letting some of the boys drive it on deserted country roads or parking lots. The tight steering and surprising acceleration needed a lot of empty space for that first driving experience.

I began making actual friendships with a few students (some of whom have maintained contact with me to the present time) in a school environment that was generally aloof and negative toward student-teacher fraternization. I allowed students to call me by my first name (not a common practice in those days) but 'Charlie' rather than 'Bill' as the teachers called me. That way, if I happened to be talking to a teacher and a student happened to call out, 'Hey Charlie', I could just ignore it and the teacher wouldn't notice the chummy relationship.

There are so many students I would like to mention, but obviously I can't mention then all and mentioning only some of them wouldn't be fair to the others. They all enriched my life just by being themselves in my classes.

However, I do have to mention Phil because he taught me a lot about how to be successful, and I have shared this with many people, including student teachers. He liked me because he was addicted to playing pool at noon hour. No, we didn't play pool together, but I was his teacher for the first class in the afternoon, and he was usually late for class. I was one of the few teachers who really believed that finishing a pool game could be more important than the first fifteen minutes of a lesson. Several years later, he became a teacher and then a school counselor in Portage. We had occasions to be together in meetings with principals and parents and I was curious as to how he made such a positive impression on everyone (except me, of course). So he told me about his working for the hydroelectric power company before coming to the school system. It went something like this:

"The first thing to do after you have driven out to where the repair is to made is to leave the truck doors open, take out your tool boxes and leave them open with tools spread out on the roadside. Anyone driving by, including supervisors, will observe that you are working."

"OK. So what does this have to do with a meeting in the school?" I asked.

"When I go to a meeting, I always have a briefcase. The first thing I do is to put it on the desk. Then I open it and take out some papers, and look at them as if I am refreshing my memory about something. Then we can start the meeting. They are impressed because they think I am organized and know what I am doing."

'Little Portage' was a popular gathering and snacking place on the outskirts of Portage. I didn't know anyone, so I began going there soon after school started. I became friends with one of the more obviously attractive waitresses and got into the habit of picking Sharon up after work and driving her home. We went swimming at Delta (the nearby beach/cottage resort on lake Manitoba) a couple of times. It is fortunate nothing serious had developed in our relationship because it ended abruptly one day at school. I noticed a group of Grade 12 students blocking the hallway because the teacher hadn't arrived to unlock their classroom door.

Being a helpful fellow, I worked my way through the group and was unlocking the door when I heard a familiar voice, "Thanks, Charlie."

You guessed it. It was Sharon. It had never occurred to me she might be a student. Maybe we should have spent more time talking.

I was 'adopted' by Milt, Russ and their mother, Clara. They had moved to Portage about the time I did and when I met them they had a house but still no furniture. It was fun seeing them slowly fill up the house, complete with the big stereo system popular at that time. I also enjoyed spending time helping Milt work on his light blue coupe of questionable lineage.

Milt and I did a fast (in both time and speed) tenting tour straight south almost to the Mexican border, then to the west coast for Disneyland and home.

Later, when I went to Stanford, I left the Triumph with Russ to look after. Fortunately, the car couldn't tell me any tales, but rumor has it that there were some stories to tell.

As seven years rolled by, I came to realize that for a lot of the students their lack of academic success generally was not so much from lack of ability as from emotional, personal or personality difficulties. When the provincial Department of Education decided to encourage more guidance and counseling in the schools by offering a bursary for teachers to take a master's program, Grand Forks was the closest university with an appropriate program. I enrolled, and Wilma and I set off to the United States for me to begin my program.

We had a self-contained suite in a lady's basement. We had just nicely adjusted to our new life when a French teaching opportunity became available beginning the last week in September. It was in Arborg, a 2-hour drive north of Winnipeg. From then until Christmas, Wilma would meet the Arborg school principal in Winnipeg on Sunday night to go with him to Arborg. Then I would drive to Grand Forks for my week of classes. When the weekend came, we would reverse the process. We would meet in Winnipeg, have a nice dinner, and then drive home to Portage.

In January, Wilma and I returned to Grand Forks. She took some creative ceramics and fancy knitting classes while I was working on my thesis and finishing my course work. Wilma was expecting our first child, Ken, at the end of July and I had planned my program so

I would be finished mid-July. It worked out well, except for a minor glitch described in a later chapter. We were both home when Ken arrived on the 23rd.

While I had been away getting my master's degree in counseling and psychology, the School Division hired its first Superintendent of Schools. I had left under the impression from the School Board that I would be Supervisor of Counseling (or Guidance, or some such title). When I returned I discovered I might be called Supervisor but there was no counseling program for me to supervise and, in fact, no interest in having one. I made a compromise and became Guidance Counselor at PCI and was authorized to call myself Supervisor of Student Services (my toehold into a divisional counseling program) with a very modest extra pay allowance.

One of the aspects of the high school program was arranging a once-a-year field trip to Winnipeg so students could visit facilities offering post-secondary opportunities in education and employment. It took a lot of time and effort to set up the contacts and arrange bus routes (there were hundreds of students and dozens of places for the tours), but the day itself was pretty easy for me. There were always teachers to ride the bus and act as guides. The students knew where they needed to be and when. If they missed a bus it was their problem, not mine. If they had to phone a parent to come and pick them up or to take a Greyhound bus back to Portage, it wouldn't be a big problem. At least that is what I told them and I guess they believed me. To my knowledge nobody ever missed a bus. But then, I wouldn't have necessarily known, would I?

For five years, I served as counselor in both high schools (at different times) and then as junior high counselor for all the junior high schools. I always tried to leave a vacancy to be filled when I moved so that gradually the junior and senior high schools all had counseling programs.

There were young people in Portage who used drugs like LSD, pot and especially hash. Harder drugs were common in Winnipeg and there was concern they would reach the high schools in Portage.

Thanks to my years of teaching, and my penchant for getting to know young people and their lives, I knew all the drug dealers and major drug purchasers in Portage, their *modus operandi,* and their suppliers. The first step in my drug control program was to meet each of the local dealers one-on-one, usually over a beer, and let them know that if I ever saw one of them in a school, on the school grounds or even near the school grounds, I would have to call the RCMP (Royal Canadian Mounted Police) and tell them everything I knew (which was a lot). They stayed away and out of sight.

However, drugs did sneak into the schools via student users. As in most schools, we had a drug information program and provision to help those who asked for assistance. A problem arose when a couple of student told me the hash suppliers in Winnipeg were lacing hash with small amounts of heroin to make it more addictive. I checked with the local RCMP and they told me they were aware of the problem but didn't know how extensive it was.

We set up an agreement that I could purchase small amounts of hash from students or on the street and turn it over to them for analysis. I would then quietly announce in classes whenever there was a problem with the current supply. Needless to say, this was an informal (as in, secret) program. I'm sure if some administrators had known they would have opposed it on the grounds that I was encouraging hash use by saying when it was safe. The students understood I could never tell them if what they were buying or using was safe. I could only tell them when I knew it wasn't. It also made a major point that they needed to think about what they were doing.

One effective lesson came about by accident. A former student (actually, he was the person who had introduced me to pot many years earlier by inviting me to one of his frequent pot parties) came to me and asked if he could talk to my students about the dangers of drug use. Being somewhat psychic, (or at least observant), I suspected he had returned to Portage recently to set himself up as an informal dealer and was looking to enlist users. I was sure of it when he said he would have to speak to the students without having me present.

His complexion was pallid and teeming with blemishes; his mouth moved constantly and his eyes were squinty; his voice, hands and whole body shook; he had a major face twitch; and he bounced around like a flea on speed. I decided that if he wanted to be 'poster boy' for drug use, I should let him.

So I took a chance and gave him my classes for the day. I checked with the class after my former student's first performance. The response was along the lines of:

"Where on earth did you find that guy? He told us he'd been using drugs for years and they hadn't done him any harm at all. But he's a total wreck. If he's what drug use does to you, no thank you. He said pot never leads to anything stronger, and then he says he's been on every drug there is."

I assumed they got a message. I firmly believed that young people can make good decisions it they have all the facts. Not all school administers believed that.

Unfortunately, personal counseling was gradually phasing out and being replaced with vocational counseling.

I had one guidance counselor say to me:

"I don't know why you bother with personal counseling. It is so much harder than vocational."

I thought it was also more rewarding both personally and for society.

In 1972, the Portage School Division decided they should have a Special Education Coordinator to assist with the implementation of Manitoba Legislation requiring handicapped individuals be placed in the 'least restrictive' settings for education and living. And so I became 'Coordinator of Special Education & Student Services'. In this role, I organized the activities of specialists such as psychologist, social worker, speech therapist, and other resource personnel.

My job could be summarized as getting students with any form of handicap integrated into the regular school program as much as was feasible. In short, I had to negotiate between parents who wanted a more 'normal' setting for their child and with schools who did not want that kind of person in their schools.

As one principal said, "The wheelchair leaves muddy tracks on our carpet."

It was not an easy job.

Up until this time, I had been changing my educational role about every seven years. I liked that. I had discovered that after about five years I would be finding shortcuts and easier ways to do things. I would start to lose my enthusiasm and feeling of adventure. My stint in Special Education didn't end until 1986. I tried unsuccessfully to get out of the position several times. Fourteen years was too long in that role.

My last six years in the division were as 'Divisional Consultant for Talented/Gifted', replacing the person who had started the program a few years earlier. We followed Renzulli's philosophy and programs (described briefly on page 159), which were based mostly on teacher support and encouragement.

I did set up and taught evening high school courses for talented and gifted students, which ran one night a week for three years. One was called, 'Societal Issues'.

I began the course by saying, "I have no information to give you. It is up to you to share your knowledge and opinions with each other. I am just here to guide you."

We discussed and debated topics of importance to them in a civilized and thoughtful manner—totally unlike our Federal Parliament during question period.

I tried to teach them precision in language usage, so they would avoid saying things like, "How could our hockey team lose?" Obviously, by putting the puck into the net fewer times than the other team. Was this really what you were saying?

Or, "Do you believe in UFO's?" A person has to believe there have been observations of moving things in the sky, which have not been identified. Did they mean to ask, "Do you believe in extraterrestrial beings?"

I also ran a Saturday morning Science course for gifted elementary school age students. We dealt with observation, thinking and a scientific approach to practical problems . . . like making a jet propelled cars with sticks and a balloon. One time, the class included a pre-reading student and a junior high student together. Because the class was based on observation, ideas and thinking, rather than information, age was not important. Everyone could contribute equally.

I started teaching computer science and programming in the 'traditional languages' of BASIC, FORTRAN and COBOL languages about 1970 because my son, Ken, was ready to learn them. I thought I might as well make it available to all high school students. Ken was in Grade 6 and most of the other students were in Grade 11 or 12. I needed Ken there for the many times when my knowledge wasn't as good as his. After their initial surprise, the students accepted Ken as a midget equal.

We used cardboard cards with columns of ovals to be pencil marked to select letters or numbers. Then the cards had to be sent away to a card reader connected to a computer to have the program run. It was a slow process, but it was fascinating to be on the cutting edge of the new computer technology. When personal computers became available and could run programs such as C++, I moved into teaching this language. As you might have guessed, I had little knowledge of this computer language, but I had read that they were best learned through experience. The students succeeded in writing complex programs with a minimum of teacher assistance.

About 1978, when Commodore, Radio Shack, and Apple started making personal computers a reality for ordinary people, I became interested in making computer power available for education and communication purposes. Unfortunately, because many verbally handicapped people are also physically handicapped to the extent that they cannot operate a keyboard, they were unable to make use of this new technology. I found a company in the United States that was making pressure-sensitive computer keyboards. I begin customizing them by using a plastic overlay with holes cut in it for a person's fingers to go through and press the individual keys. The software enabled the user to print words on the monitor—for some this was their first ability to communicate.

A few weeks after being set up with the system, one non-verbal young man typed on the screen for his social worker to read, 'i am being abused'. They investigated and removed him from his foster home placement. The word board he previously used didn't have the right options for his message.

For several years I distributed them widely in Canada and to several locations in the United States, mostly to schools and hospitals. Just for the record, the company was called, 'Cacti Computer Services'. I assumed no other company would have that name, and so it saved the cost and nuisance of doing a name search.

After my official retirement from teaching, I started supervising practicum experiences in various schools for student teachers primarily from Brandon University and the University of Manitoba. It is an enjoyable way to maintain contact with the schools, students and educational changes.

A lot has changed in education over the years, but the one thing that has stayed constant is the dedication of the teachers and the delightful enthusiasm and originality of the students. It continues to keep me young . . . in spirit if not in body.

***

~ Cause Or Effect? ~

I was sitting in the staff room after a day of meetings and discussions in one of the schools. The principal had called me to the school as part of my duties as Supervisor of Student Services to mediate a problem between the parents of a student, the student and the school.

I was having a cup of coffee before going home when one of the older lady teachers sat down across from me and fixed me with a steely stare.

She said, with the utmost sincerity: "Every time you come to our school you cause a problem. Why don't you just stay away and leave us alone?"

I got up, washed my coffee cup and left. What could I say?

***

~ Dealing With Problems ~

I was struggling with a computer program that wouldn't do what I wanted, and asked Ken's advice.
Me: "How do I fix this bug in my program."
Ken: "Just say it isn't a bug, it's a feature."

Ken says this isn't an original line, but it has helped me to put a lot of my non-computer problems into perspective.

***

~ Friends ~

Me, in class: "What do people in this place do for recreation?"
James: "There is five-pin bowling."
Me: "I've never tried that, but I'd be afraid of scraping my finger nails on the lane."
James was waiting for me at the door after the class dismissed: "Do you want me to teach you to bowl?"
Me: "Sure, if you really want to."
We went bowling a couple of times a week at about 5 PM when I would have finished at school.
Fast-forward a couple of months. James and I had a major confrontation in class and I ended up sending him to the office. He returned to class and sat down without comment. I was at the door as the class filed out.
As he passed me he paused: "See you for bowling at 5." It wasn't a question —just a reminder.
I never could get past my need to turn my hand at the last moment (to protect my fingernails) with the consequent spin toward a gutter. I did learn to compensate for the spin . . . somewhat . . . by aiming for the gutter.
James was very kind and patient with his inept student.

***

~ Guilty Conscience ~

On our yearly field day trip to Winnipeg there were two students who lived in a small rural town outside Portage who needed a ride back home. It was simpler for me to drive them rather than have them take the bus.
It had been a hot, thirsty day.
Student: "I don't suppose we could stop for a beer before we go home, could we?"

Me: *"Sounds good to me. Would it be OK with your parents?"*

Student: *"Yeah. He lets us drink anytime we want, so long as we don't drink his beer."*

Me: *"OK. But just one."*

Based on this rather sparse parental approval, we stopped at a small hotel and went into the beverage room. There were only a few people scattered around the room. The three of us sat down and ordered a glass of draft beer each.

We were about half through our glasses of beer when a middle-aged man in a business suit came over, pulled up a chair and sat down as if he belonged there. *"Hi fellows. I see you are drinking draft."*

At this point I was trying to come up with a plan of action. I thought he was a liquor commission inspector, and I was there with two underage drinkers. I wasn't doing anything wrong (they had bought the beer, not me), but they could be in big trouble. The three of us exchanged quizzical looks but that didn't help.

Before I had time to formulate any kind of plan, he asked, *"Have you tried Molson's new beer? It's way better than draft."*

We all replied emphatically in unison: *"No."*

We weren't going to admit to anything. We wouldn't have even admitted that three glasses on the table belonged to us.

The man said: *"Well, you should."*

He motioned to the waiter who brought three bottles for us.

As the man got up to leave he said: *"He'll bring you more if you ask. I'm sure you will like it. Been nice meeting you."*

Obviously, he was a salesman for the brewery and was happy to convert three young guys to a lifetime of his product.

We probably drank more than we had intended. I don't remember much more of the trip home, except having to stop by the roadside twice.

***

~ Hopelessness ~

One of my former students, who had just been released from Stony Mountain Penitentiary, came to talk to me. He was thin, strung-out and with a major prison pallor. He didn't know what to do now that he was out *of jail. He hadn't finished high school, had no marketable skills or contacts with any aspect of the work force, and no friends.*

He said he needed to get back into jail because it was the only place he knew how to behave or what to do.

I tried to be helpful, but I really didn't know what to suggest.

He asked if there was anything I could do to get him back into jail.

I couldn't even help him with that.

***

~ No Problem ~

School Superintendent: "We can't start that program until we get approval for the $20,000 funding."

Me: "We will get the funding."

Superintendent: " What if we start the program and don't get the funding?"

Me: "Then just take it out of my salary —$100 a month for the next 20 years."

Fortunately, the funding was approved, because I only taught 8 more years.

***

~ Help - Get Me Out of This ~

A grade 10 student came to see me in my office: "I need to tell you something."

Me: "It's confidential unless you are going to tell me about something illegal that is going to happen. In that case, I would have to report it to the RCMP."

Student: "Some friends and I are planning to rob a store."

Me: "If you tell me anything more, I'll have to report it to the RCMP."

The student continued to tell me where and when it would happen.

Me (as the student was leaving): "You do realize I will have to report this to the RCMP."

After he left, I phoned the RCMP and reported the information with the suggestion it likely wouldn't happen because the student knew I was reporting it.

The robbery did take place several days later at a different location, but without the student being involved in it.

***

~ The Devil Made Me Do It ~

I was sitting in the back row of the Grade 12 class, observing and writing a report on the student teacher who was teaching the class.

Student (sitting in the desk beside me): "Who are you?"

Me: "I work for Brandon University. I check on the learning process in the class."

Student: "What are you doing?"

Me: "Writing a report."

Student: "Oh."

I had noticed the student's behavior earlier. He was an obviously bright youngster, bored in school, and with a lot of excessive energy to burn off.

Student: "Who is the report on?"

Me (wanting him to go away): "It's on you."

He looked startled and turned away from me to watch the teacher. At this point, the devil in my head got the best of me. I took an extra blank form and started filling in the headings with comments about him— things like, 'a bright student, but needs to pay more attention in class' and 'needs to spend less time fooling around and more time applying himself to the tasks at hand' and 'a showoff and disruption in class'.

Student: "Do you show this to the university?"

Me: "Yep."

Student: "Does it determine whether or not I get accepted there?"

I shrugged and kept writing. "How do you spell your last name?"

He told me and I carefully printed it on the form. For the rest of the class he was the perfect student— quiet, cooperative, and answering questions seriously.

At the end of the class, he leaned over to me. "Are you really sending that to Brandon University?"

I relented. "No. I was just kidding you. My report is on the student teacher."

He was too relieved to be annoyed at me. I showed my report on him to the classroom teacher and she thought it was hilarious.

She asked me if she could have it to show his mother, who, unbeknownst to me, was also a teacher in the school.

***

- A Modern Approach To Class Control -

Classroom teacher to student teacher: "Are you going to be able to handle this group if I am not here?

Student teacher (loud enough for the students to hear): "If I crash and burn, I'll take as many of them with me as I can."

He had no problems with the somewhat horrified students.

***

STAYING IN A CASTLE

VIEW FROM OUR ROOM   **OUR BEDROOM**

There Is Life Outside School

In my third year teaching in Portage la Prairie, I was on the divisional salary negotiating team with a young teacher named Wilma. After the meetings, we would often go to the Mayfair Polynesian Room for a Mai Tai. It didn't get any further than that because it was usually on the same day as her CGIT (Canadian Girls in Training) church group. The closest we ever got to real dating was our trips to Winnipeg for a seafood platter at the Ivanhoe restaurant.

Wilma and I got engaged, much to the relief of my brother and his wife, who thought I would never get married. Now they could stop worrying about me. When we visited them in Regina prior to our engagement, Joan, Cliff's wife, took me aside and encouraged me to not let Wilma get away. It was good advice. We had still not been on a real date. We tried a few times to go on a date or to spend a quiet evening by ourselves but seemed always to have someone else added onto our twosome which made it more like a party than a date. Marriage seemed like the best way to go if we were going to be able to spend any private time together.

One night when we were sitting in the Triumph, I decided to make the big move.

In my most seductive voice, I suggested, "Will you marry me?"

Wilma replied, almost in her teacher voice, "I have no intention of getting married, and if I did, it wouldn't be to someone like you."

I wasn't sure if I should pursue the question of what kind of a person she would marry, or what kind of person she thought I was.

So I just ignored the comment and thought to myself, "Well, I guess it's going to take longer than I thought."

We became engaged (without a ring) two weeks later.

We continued our non-dating until July when Wilma flew to Montreal to take a French language course at McGill University. I stayed in Portage to mark departmental final exams in Winnipeg (I was short of money at the time …as usual).

When I finished marking, I hopped on a Greyhound Bus and set off to Montreal. It wasn't that I was following her. I just had a sudden urge to visit Montreal. If I had thought to check how far away it was or how long it would take to get there, I might have taken a faster means of transportation. But then, I was too busy marking exam papers to plan my life.

Thirty-six hours later I arrived in Montreal and found a rooming house with a cheap room for rent. It was just a room with a bed and a chair, not even a sink. The washroom was down the hall and around the corner. I soon discovered 'near beer'. It was unique to the province of Quebec at that time. Every grocery store sold quart-size bottles of good, cold, low alcohol beer.

I usually walked to the University in the late afternoon to meet Wilma after class. We would have dinner, walk around for a while and sit in the park. One evening we discovered that the park was considered closed after dark when a security person with a German Shepherd dog discovered us and suggested, in rapid and emphatic French, we go elsewhere. It was alright because Wilma needed to get back to her residence to be ready for class in the morning. I walked her to the residence door and then headed back to my room. On the way, I picked up a quart or two of beer at a corner store to sip on for the evening. I never had any trouble finding a friend or two at the rooming house to keep me company…and share my beer…and carry on one-way conversations in French. I was a good listener.

Wilma had made plans to go on tour overseas to join a couple of her girl friends immediately after her course ended. I saw her to the airport, kissed her goodbye, told her I thought God meant us to be together, and she flew off to find her foreign knight in shining armor riding a white horse. At least, that was what she told me. My year would be spent back in Portage teaching eager students … and being supportive to the others. I went back to my room and had a couple of beers with my recently made friends whose names I never knew. They were nice guys and I did improve my spoken French a little. The next morning I hopped a bus for another day-and-a-half trip back to Portage.

Wilma and I exchanged letters by mail, which was a painfully slow method of communication. She phoned her parents (and thus me, if she called at dinner time) occasionally. She toured Holland, East and West Germany, the British Isles, France, Italy, and Russia.

On the ship from St. Petersburg, she was invited to be the guest at the captain's table. Since it was a Russian ship, there was a lot of caviar and dancing. But the captain didn't steal her heart, and docking in London ended that interlude.

While Wilma was overseas, I went to Winnipeg and purchased an engagement ring. We had previously looked at rings so I sort of knew what she would like, and I knew her ring size from a goldstone ring I had bought her when I first decided she was the one for me. I couldn't bring the ring back with me because it needed to be sized. When she arrived in Winnipeg the timing wasn't right to pick up the ring before I met her at the airport so we went back to Portage without the ring.

While she was away, she had decided she wanted to get engaged. I wasn't making any move towards giving her a ring, so she dropped 'hints'. I ignored the hints and they kept getting less and less subtle. I arranged for us to go to Winnipeg for shopping and dinner at Rae and Jerry's. At this point she might have become suspicious because Rae and Jerry's was not our usual kind of dining place. It was expensive, old-fashioned and formal, and let's face it, that does not describe me very well. We went shopping, and on the pretense of going to the washroom (what would we guys ever do without the pretense of a washroom break to escape from our girl friend) I got away and picked up the ring. Before we went in for dinner I proposed and she accepted the ring. She even managed to act surprised. We went back there for dinner on our 25th Anniversary and it looked exactly the same. Some things never change. It is still a popular restaurant for the older, richer crowd. We were married in Portage on July 18, 1964 with two ministers officiating. It never hurts to have a backup minister, but neither of us tried to escape.

We found a nice little 'starter home' in Portage. It was a 1½ story, 3 bedroom, 'wartime' house. It was within easy walking distance from PCI where we taught and an elementary school for our kids-to-be. We didn't shop around much because we thought we would probably be moving soon anyway. Our house shared a fence with our next-door neighbor. She was a lovely lady to have as a neighbor, except that she kept a very neat lawn, a small tidy, weed-free vegetable garden and a little patch of sweet peas. I was never able to pass muster in keeping up with her.

However, she did once say that I 'hung out a good wash'.

There was never a weed out of place. She taught piano, which made it convenient for both our children to get a solid foundation in piano and a love of music. We lived there for 28 years before moving one block over.

When we did get around to moving, we only moved one street over and could carry most of our things just across the street and down the back lane. The movers for our fridge and freezer were used to being able to catch their breath on the drive from the person's old house to their new one. With us, it was less than two minutes.

We had more than our share of parties over the years. We had fondue parties when they were popular, and wine and cheese parties. I was never much of a wine drinker but I used to love picking out an interesting variety of wines, and cheeses which in those days were cheaper by far than they are now.

The Portage School Division accidentally attracted a teacher (Georges) and his wife (Josette) all the way from France to join our staff. He thought from the name that Portage la Prairie must be a French community. It isn't. I was glad to see I was not the only one to make major moves without doing all the research. He came to one of our wine and cheese parties and we played 'guess where the wine is from'. Wilma and I didn't succeed in guessing much beyond whether it was red or white and what the percentage of alcohol was. It turns out his family in France owned a winery. He was able not only to identify the country and region but could tell the condition of the vineyard and the history of its grapes. Of course, he might have been making up half of what he said and we'd have had no way of knowing. Even if he were, it was impressive. He and his wife were always an entertaining addition to our parties.

Even as a young child, Anita liked to take the easiest route. She wanted to communicate before she was ready to talk, so she invented her own system of making an 'hhhuuhhh' sound and then inflecting it, like you might do to make it sound like a 'yes' or a 'no'. Her 'I don't know' was unmistakable and frequently used. In high school her friends would ask Anita questions just to hear her distinctive *'I'd'll'no'* response.

Ken, on the other hand, didn't talk until he was 3-years-old. He was waiting until he could speak in correct, complete sentences. In most things, Ken preferred to wait until he was sure of himself. He didn't like to practice in public. Anita and Ken got along well with each other as children, with the notable exceptions of trading collected stamps and playing Boggle.

Because Wilma and I were both teachers, we liked to travel. After our children were born we bought a 'normal' car so we could take them with us on road trips to Vancouver, the east coast and the United States. We did some tenting with my old but still sturdy tent with all the usual experiences associated with tents. As the children got bigger, the tent seemed to get smaller. We bought an old school bus and I removed the seats converting it into a camper. The back nine feet were the master bedroom with a hide-a-bed, which could be folded up to make a nice play area for Ken and Anita. It was complete with all the comforts of home and served us nobly until the price of gas made motels with a swimming pool look more attractive.

And then, we also purchased a cottage at Delta, 20 minutes north of Portage, on Lake Manitoba. We bought it sort of by default. Wilma's parents had had a cottage when Wilma was growing up and they were talking about getting a cottage again. They had found a nice one at a reasonable price just before Gard (Wilma's dad) died suddenly. So what could we do? We bought it, even though we had a camper bus at the time.

For a couple of years we had a cottage with a camper bus parked in its back yard. One winter we had it parked in the lane beside our house for a teenager to live in, when the Children's Aid couldn't find a home placement for him

The cottage was a great place for our children. Our next-door neighbor, Clarice, was a resource teacher in the school system with two girls and a boy a bit older than ours. Delta had a perfect beach for children. It was shallow at the edge and sloped gently for many yards before getting deep enough to really swim. Our children and hers played together and spent hours on the beach making castles in the sand. Her son, Allen, taught Ken (and us) how to make drip castles from wet sand. The Brown's cottage was an A-frame with a 'fireman' pole through a hole between the two levels. Anita in particular loved sliding down and never hurt herself ... at least not enough for her to let us notice. One time, or so I was told *many* years later, Ken accidentally knocked Anita down the hole from the second floor, but Allen was there to catch her. Ken thought it was a pretty fun activity and tried to do it again . . . but Anita was smarter the second time.

It was when we were at Delta that I had cause to make my first trip to the hospital since having my tonsils out at age 24. I was mowing the grass around our outdoor 'biffy' across the road from our cottage. The grass was a bit high and the push mower was balky. To help it along I gave it a push with my foot. The whooshy sound made me think I had run over a piece of cardboard, but when I looked down I saw it was my shoe that had slipped under the mower. I felt no pain in walking back to the cottage. I sat on the step and started to remove the remnants of my shoe. I had started to remove my blood-soaked sock when it occurred to me that my toes might come off with the sock, and I didn't know how I would carry a severed toe or two on the 20-minute drive to the Portage hospital emergency room. The big toe had a chip out of the bone but other than that it was just fine except I had to use crutches for a few weeks—stairs became a new experience for me.

Years later, Delta was again the scene of my next medical problem, and my first contact with our present doctor, Dr. Lou. I woke up in the early morning hours with a sharp pain in the left side of my chest.

It became very painful if I tried to take a deep breath, so I followed the advice I would have given the children—I didn't take a deep breath.

I waited until after everyone was up (why ruin their night's sleep) before suggesting to Wilma that I thought I should visit the hospital. I was on a hospital bed with an oxygen tube in my nose when a young man (he looked to be about 17 years old), clad in a white hospital gown, came in to examine me. He had a, roundish, clean-shaven, youthful face.

My initial thought was, "Good grief. Why do I have a high school 'work education program' student coming in to look at me?"

Dr. Lou asked me if I could take a deep breath. I wasn't sure what answer to give. There were only two possible answers, 'yes' or 'no'. But it was like those infernal 'true' or 'false' questions on an exam. Neither answer would be completely correct. Yes, I could take a deep breath but I was sure it would kill me if I did. So really, the answer should be, no. I don't recall whether or not I explained all this to him—probably not.

"Does that hurt?" he asked, pushing in just the right place to elicit a reaction that made a verbal response totally redundant.

He gave me a prescription and sent me on my way.

My (non-verbal) reaction was, "Yeah. As if that's going to cure my heart attack. I want to see a real doctor."

Twenty-four hours later I was 100% cured. He explained later that it was just a virus infection on the end of one of my ribs—not something that would ever have occurred to me. I still think he had no business figuring that out with just one question and a well placed poke. I must admit I have had immense respect for his wisdom and skill since that time. Besides, he likes old cars, and that counts for a lot. Granted, they are American cars, but then, no one is perfect.

Over the years, he has poked, prodded and tapped me in what appear to be randomly chosen places. Somehow, he seems to know what it all means and has succeeded in keeping me healthy for years. He also knows me well enough to know I will to almost anything to avoid taking medication. When my sugar level and cholesterol level were getting high, he drew me a diagram explaining how those levels and my blood pressure were indicating I was getting close to needing medication.

"What should I do about a diet," I asked him.

"If it's worth eating, then you can't eat it," he replied.

It was good advice.

I must mention the time I fell off a chair and threw my shoulder out of joint—and no, I was sober at the time. I was given a shot of morphine, twice, and was a bit light-headed. I was wheeled to the X-Ray lab over my protestations that I could walk. When I arrived, I hopped off the gurney, walked over to the machine, stood there for my X-ray, and then hopped back onto the gurney. Someone must have told Dr. Lou that I was not as sedated as I needed to be. Back in the examination room, I recall Dr. Lou coming in through the door with a vial and syringe in his hand.

"This should work for you," he said.

And that was the last thing I remembered until I woke up much later. I had no memory of his walking toward me from the doorway, let alone being injected, or the apparent pain —Wilma says he told her to leave the room because there would be significant yelling and screaming from me— while he was forcing my shoulder back into position. That was a clear, obvious example of retrograde memory loss—one in which events *prior* to a trauma are forgotten. I can understand anterograde amnesia (loss of memory of events *after* the trauma) because you are unconscious and hence the events just do not register in your brain. But I find memory loss of events you have already experienced to be strange because you have experienced the events and maybe even responded to them.

So, how do they get erased retroactively? I have this small germ of a theory that maybe it is like the time-delay on live television in which the broadcast is electronically delayed for a few seconds in order to delete profanity and such. Maybe all of life is on a twenty-second time-delay. I chose twenty seconds because I estimate that to be about the length of time for Dr. Lou to have walked from the door to me and get the injection into my system. Try thinking about that for a while—or at least for twenty seconds.

Our children both had birthdays in July so it was logical to have the parties at Delta where there was lots of sandy space, water in which to play and a wood fire for wieners and marshmallows. We would fill our camper bus with the guests in Portage and drive them to Delta.

After one of the parties for Ken, at which I had taken movies, played 'fish' over a hanging blanket, supervised races and had (I thought) been generally front-and-center, I was tucking Ken into bed.

With his eyes mostly closed, he looked up at me and said, "I had a lovely party, Daddy. Were you there?"

That pretty well sums up our boy, Ken. He always threw himself into whatever he was doing so thoroughly he didn't notice his surroundings. He still doesn't drink alcohol, smoke or swear. He just never found time for that sort of nonsense.

Both our children got on a fast track out of our home and each left around age 16. We tried not to take it personally. Ken was always ahead of his time in school. He liked school by just ignoring everything around him. He took Grade 8 and 9 in one year, moving up midyear. The top Grade 9 students were relieved to find that they would still be able to win the academic awards because the school created a special award for Ken and maintained the other awards for the rest of the grade. We were very pleased that they took this step to clear the path for Ken and avoid hard feelings with his classmates. He then did Grades 10, 11 and 12 in two years by taking courses by correspondence. He had decided he wanted to get out of high school and into some meaningful education as quickly as possible.

Ken always had a great ability to set priorities and, although he worked constantly, he made time for his piano, playing sax in the school jazz band and playing badminton. He graduated with the Governor General's Award (just like his mother), and headed off to the University of Waterloo, in Ontario. He chose to go there because it had an excellent reputation in Mathematics and Computer Science.

Sometimes Anita says she is lazy, but I prefer to think of it as being efficient. She likes to shop for clothing in the marked down section, not because it saves money, but because it cuts down on the number of decisions. Anita says her taking the easiest route is in the Taoist way of a stream finding its path. It flows along the easiest route.

When Anita chose a musical instrument in addition to the piano, she decided on the oboe because no one else in her grade played one and thus she would be assured of a place on band trips. The oboe is arguably one of the most difficult orchestral instruments to play, which would seem to contradict my earlier statement that she tended to chose the easiest route. It is, however, one of the lightest and easiest instruments to carry around (I guess the piccolo wasn't an option), so I rest my case. I like to think Anita took after me. After all, she did place third in a local photo beauty contest when she was three years old—and my mother always said I was a cute boy until I turned four. Anita just stayed cuter longer than I did.

Somewhere, Anita got the idea to attend the Royal Conservatory of Music in Toronto the same summer that Wilma decided to take a real-life immersion in French in Jonquière in Quebec. It may or may not be a coincidence that this was the same time that we were serving as a volunteer Children's Aid home for a teenager who had run himself out of homes that would take him. I decided this would be a good excuse for me to take a bit of a holiday by flying there with her to help her get established in the university residence. The University of Toronto was not in session making inexpensive accommodation available nearby.

We had a lot of fun looking at cars in parking lots. I rented a tiny compact car for the week and whenever we encounter a Porsche on the street I would race it from one stoplight to the next. I rarely won, and then it was only because I was lucky in guessing which lane to be in. The Porsche driver probably didn't even know he was in a race.

It was a nice bonding experience for me, and I experienced pangs of regret when my week was up and I had to fly home leaving Anita at the mercy of the big city.

After I had left, Ken planned to have Anita visit him in Waterloo for a weekend. He arranged for a friend (whom Anita didn't know) to pick up Anita on the sidewalk in front of a particular subway station in Toronto. As requested, Anita was waiting on the sidewalk at the appointed time when a car drove up.

The driver rolled down the window, and called out, "Get in."

Anita, having been brought up to be obedient, hopped into the car and they drove off. Fortunately, it was the right fellow. Anita did admit later that she should have checked to see if the driver actually was someone who knew who she was. But then, if you have a guardian angel to look after you, little details like this are looked after for you.

Anita didn't enjoy school much. Unlike Ken, she took school seriously and that can be a bad scene for a thoughtful youngster. She got good grades but didn't think she deserved them because the work was so easy. This made her feel vaguely guilty and also she hated the attitude some of the other students had toward her high marks. At the end of Grade 10, Wilma and I decided Anita would do better in a more challenging school system. St. John's-Ravenscourt (SJR) in Winnipeg was an obvious choice as a school with very high academic standards. The residence at SJR had been 'boys only' up until two years before Anita went there, so girls were still a bit of a novelty for them.

In Grade 9 and 10 it was evident that Anita had high ability in Math. She placed at or near the top of various provincial Math contests in Grade 10 and 11. The school system reacted to this by having her sit in the hallway to work on her own, and they just ignored her in the area of Math because she was good at it. Consequently, by the end of Grade 10 she had not actually attended any Math classes since Grade 8.

Anita needed to have her official Mathematics standings in order to fit into the SJR program. The program at SJR was generally a grade level more advanced than the public system so she would need to have her Grade 11 Mathematics to be on a par with other students. I arranged with the Department of Education to get the whole year of Mathematics correspondence course at once so she could go through it during the summer. I also had to arrange a special sitting for her to write the final exam so she would have a final mark for SJR when school started. It helped that I had done this sort of thing before with special students in my regular work in the Portage School Division. The transition to the academic rigor of SJR had its traumatic moments but was ultimately successful academically and personally for her.

Anita made some good friends in her two years there, including the fine young man she would eventually marry—although it did take them 7 more years to actually get engaged because they liked to discuss things thoroughly. As a married couple they still don't make decisions without discussing all possible options . . . and often a few impossible ones.

Travel has always been a major part of our family life. When Ken was 8 and Anita 5, we flew overseas to London with my seventy-eight-year-old mother. She was in good health but needed a cane (except sometimes when we left a restaurant she didn't realize she needed it until we had traveled several miles away).

We rented a car in London and drove north to Sherwood Forest to fulfill Anita's dream of seeing the area made famous by the legends of Robin Hood. We saw Little John's grave, thatched roofs (even one on a bird house) and a 600-year-old hollow tree like the one in which Robin Hood used to hold meetings.

Then on to Wales, stopping at *Caernarvon* Castle, which extended Ken's fascination with drawing the maze of train tracks in a rail yard to drawing schematics of the castle turrets, passages, and stairs. Escher would have been proud of him.

Ireland was the main focus of our trip partly because Wilma's mother, Frances, always maintained she was Irish (her brother, Hugh, always maintained he was Scottish even though they had the same parents). Ireland was just what one would expect. It was green, friendly, scenic, and often was moist with the gentle Irish mist. We kissed the Blarney stone, went to the Cliffs of Moher (much to my mother's delight), kissed the Blarney Stone, climbed the Cashel tower and Ken rode a little Irish donkey. Ken and Anita tried, unsuccessfully, to herd a flock of sheep on the grounds of an abandoned monastery. I didn't offer any advice, but a Collie dog would have been very helpful.

We went to Bunratty Castle for their medieval banquet. It was a great show with costumes, eating good food with our fingers, being threatened with time in the dungeon and a lot of laughter for everyone. My mother was delighted to receive a compliment on how elegant she looked in her long gown. We did the full tourist tour of Southern Ireland.

Anita had her 5th birthday in Wales and Ken had his 8th in Ireland. Whenever we had traveled in the United States, we would 'collect' states, often making small detours or crossing a bridge just to catch the corner of a new one.

On this trip, Anita wanted to have visited as many countries as she was years old. On the way back to London, we detoured briefly into

Scotland because, if you counted the United States, Scotland made up her five. Young people make life so much more fun.

The day we were leaving London for home I think Ken would have gladly stayed behind if he could have lived in the London Museum, but he stoically accepted his fate of going back to Canada.

After Ken's first year at the University of Waterloo, the four of us went on another trip overseas. We felt that Ken, at age 17, was too young to work for the summer and in another year he would have his own life and be too old to want to travel with his family. We decided to head overseas and tour Europe by car.

We (mostly me) felt an air-conditioned rental car would be a good idea, but soon discovered that European people don't consider air conditioning to be as essential as we did. There were few companies offering that option, and the ones that did charged as much for it as an extra as they did for the car rental itself. But it would be July, and the driving from place to place was a major part of our plans. As it turned out, there were several times we were most grateful for a supply of cool air flowing through the car.

We wanted this trip to be a memorable one. When I was planning the trip I discovered it was possible to stay in castles in Germany on the Rhine River, in Spain, and in Portugal. There were also old state-run monasteries, castles and paradores in Spain and pousadas in Portugal. These were rustic historic places that had been modified (slightly) for tourist accommodation. We never knew what to expect, other than they would be very interesting, steeped in history and situated well outside the cities. The prices were very reasonable compared to a modern hotel and the ambience was astonishing. The meals were often peculiar to the region, as were the wines. One of Anita's favorite memories is of having chocolate brioches at breakfast. Making reservations in the days before the Internet was a challenge and required planning well in advance. The postal service was slow but telephoning to a foreign country was not very effective if the people at each end of the telephone spoke a different language.

We flew to New York and from there to Paris. A train took us to Milan for our rental a car. We left Milan in a rather nice Italian car (only the fancier models had air conditioning) for an elaborate road trip through Holland, France, Liechtenstein, Switzerland, Italy, San Marino, Monaco, Spain, Portugal, Morocco (just a day trip to ride a camel and see the markets), and Andorra. We went to enough small countries and principalities to more than make up the prerequisite fourteen countries to match Anita's age. We also tried to hit most of the standard tourist places as well.

We were tempted to go to a Bull Fight in Spain, but opted for the gentler version of it in Portugal. The Portuguese version of bullfighting is almost gentle and is called 'bloodless' because they do not kill the bull in the ring as is done in Spain. The first part of the 'show' consists of a horseman dressed in a traditional costume fighting the bull from the back of a specially trained horse in order to stick a few small javelins into the back of the bull. Then one or more matadors taunt the bull with a red cape in a manner similar to the Spanish fight, except they are not armed with swords. The finale, and most exciting part, is when a group of eight men, often locals from nearby villages, storm into the ring in their ordinary work clothes, without any protection or weapons, and attempt to subdue the bull using only their own skill and strength. The sight of one of these apparently fearless men holding the bull's tail while others assaulted its body and another one throwing himself between the bull's horns to grasp its head was an exhilarating mixture of humor and fear. Although the men won by wrestling the bull to the ground in the fight we saw, it was an even battle with more likelihood of a person being hurt or killed than for any damage to the bull.

That year, Ken celebrated his 17th birthday in Paris and Anita celebrated her 14th birthday in Lisbon.

We left our car in Madrid and took a very efficient night train back to Paris.

The plane had a stopover in London but not long enough for us to get out of the airport. We flew back to New York, arriving several hours before our flight back to Winnipeg. Having nothing better to do, we went to a Broadway play.

We were dead tired from our flight from Paris to London and then New York, but fortunately the show was a loud and exuberant production of 'Dreamgirls'. I kept being startled back into wakefulness during the performance. We were glad to get back to the slower pace of Portage.

Ken and Anita had left home for university—Ken to Waterloo in Ontario, and from there to Berkeley in San Francisco; Anita to Western University in London, Ontario. I decided this would be a good time for me to decide what I wanted to do when I grew up.

Some people would say this was a classic case of midlife crisis. I was about the right age to have one. However, I already had a red sports car and I'd never been of the right temperament to run off with a younger woman. Besides, I had already married a young one.

My trip through life so far had been great, but I still wasn't sure where I was going. Inspired by my friend, Joe, I decided to do research for writing a novel that would include a life-style rather different from mine. San Francisco offered a wildly cosmopolitan and interesting environment. Also, Ken was living in Berkeley nearby so I would have some contact with reality.

I located a small residential hotel near the downtown area on the corner of Sutter and Larkin. It was really the second story of building with a restaurant/bar on the main floor. It seemed ideal and it was really inexpensive because they normally rented on a monthly basis. I paid my first week's rent with the loose money I happened to have in my pocket at the time. It had all I needed—a room with a bed. The clothes closet consisted of three coat hangers on the back of the only door. The room was cleaned once a week, which was more than adequate.

A heavy, locked, metal gate at street level controlled entry to the long, wide flight of stairs leading from street level to the second floor. The stairs served as an impromptu meeting place for the residents. If you sat at the top to the stairs you would eventually meet everyone as they came and went.

I thought the location was ideal because I was sure I would be safe here, even though it was a rough neighbourhood. Half a block down from the hotel there was a very ritzy, high priced hotel. I assumed anyone wanting to mug someone for money would look there and pick on a rich guy and not an obviously poor looking guy staying in a cheap hotel.

Around the corner and a block down the street was a bar frequented by a dozen flamboyantly dressed hookers who plied their trade all around the hotel where I stayed. This would mean that if someone were looking for a person to mug just for the fun of it, they would chose one of the hookers, and I would be relatively safe. I could just blend safely into the scenery.

I usually stopped in at that bar for a drink on my way home to the hotel after an afternoon of walking and sightseeing, and an evening of talking with the street people. The hookers quickly accepted me as just a friendly old guy and not a potential customer. They would kid around with each other, put on makeup and generally be themselves. They were very amusing and sometimes showed off just for the fun of it.

There was a small group of street people who hung out near my hotel. I often bought a large pizza for my supper so I would have some of it to share with them. I was their friend. One evening we were talking about the bar and the ladies of the night.

One of my friends said, "You know what they are don't you?"

"I assume they are hookers," I suggested tentatively.

"I guess you could call them that."

"What else would you call them?" I asked.

They looked at each other and laughed. "Why don't you take one home and you'll find out."

We changed the subject. I was obviously missing something here. After I left them, I stopped in at the bar and looked at my hooker buddies more critically. They were young, wore a lot of makeup, were thin and had very sexy legs. Then I noticed that their drinks were served in larger glasses than the customers, even though they were filled less than half way. The little hamster in my head started running faster to dredge up memories from my past and to put them together. Ah, men have larger hands than women. I looked more critically and observed my hooker friends all had thin waists but also very narrow hips. I signalled one of them to come and sit with me.

"I'm doing research for a book, and I'd like to ask you something, if you don't mind," I said, using the opening gambit I usually use to avoid people taking my questions too personally.

"Sure sweetie, but I could sure use a drink."

"Ok, but you'll have to answer more than one question then."

It's too bad I can't deduct drinks from my income tax as a business expense, I thought. I signalled the bartender and he brought me another beer and a large glass with two inches of pink liquid in it for my friend.

"I don't mean to be rude or anything, but are you a man?" I asked, as casually as I could muster.

I was rewarded with a sexy smile—I had braced myself for a slap—and an answer that was enough for me to assume I was right.

"Well, sweetie, there is really only one way to find out for sure now, isn't there."

I had just officially met my first transvestite, or at least, my first transvestite hooker . . . and his/her fellow transvestite hookers.

When I first came to San Francisco, Ken used to pick me up every evening and we would have dinner and see the sights of the city. After a few of his marathon 'entertain my father' sessions, I had to suggest that, much as I enjoyed his company, every night was more than I could handle. I had to do my slumming after I left him and that made it late into the night, and I wasn't as young as I used to be.

I distinctly got the impression Ken didn't really approve of my direct approach to research concerning street people. He made it very clear I was not to experiment with becoming a street beggar for a few days. My feeling, from limited experience, was that their need to be recognized as a real person often took precedence over their need for money—they usually wanted to talk if they thought I was listening. I hadn't actually told him that I was planning to play the role of street beggar for a few days so I could see what it was really like from their point of view. But then, he is an unusually perceptive person.

One evening I was standing on the corner near my hotel waiting for him when I heard a husky feminine voice behind me say, "Are you waiting for me?"

Thinking it was one of the ubiquitous transvestite hookers, I kept looking straight ahead.

"I think I'm the person you are waiting for me," the voice continued.

"No, thanks. I'm pretty sure you're not," I replied, still staring straight ahead so as to avoid eye contact.

"You are waiting for Ashley, aren't you?" the voice persisted.

I took a chance and turned around to find a very attractive young lady looking at me expectantly. I could tell she was not a transvestite. Her hands weren't large like a man's, and there were other obvious clues for someone as observant as I. It turned out that Ashley was Ken's girlfriend and he thought it would be convenient for us to meet on the corner so he could drive by to pick us both up at once.

It is almost impossible to find a parking place in San Francisco, so it really did make good sense . . . to him, anyway.

***

~ Safety By Association ~

A friend to me: " Tell me again why you think this hotel is a safe place to stay."

Me: "Suppose we are in the woods and you hear a bear nearby. You would be afraid, right?"

Friend: "Of course. If the bear chases us, we'd have to outrun it, and I don't think I can run faster than a bear."

Me: I wouldn't be afraid because I wouldn't have to outrun the bear."

Friend: "Why not?"

Me: "I'd only have to out run you."

Friend: "I guess. So?"

Me: "I just need to be around people who are more vulnerable than I am in order to be safe."

***

~ Young Love ~

The four of us were sitting around the table talking. Anita was in junior high and Ken was in high school. Anita was talking about the interpersonal relationships (gossiping, dating, fighting, etc.) among the boys and girls in the school.

Ken: "Was all this happening when I was there?"

***

Anita to Henry when they met at SJR: "I'm Anita Shirriff."

Henry: "Oh, I recognize that name. It's right below mine on the Cayley Mathematics Competition list."

Anita (to herself): "Humph."

They didn't go out on a date until other students told them they would be perfect for each other and they should go out together. They eventually got married.

***

~ We Can Only Hope ~

Wilma, her parents, Frances and Gard, and I drove her to Winnipeg for her flight to Montreal. We had some extra time so we did some 'window shopping' at a jewellery store. We saw a nice 12 place setting of fancy, gold edged dishes. They were being discontinued so all their extra items in that pattern were included at no extra cost.

Me (fishing for information): "Those are nice. Maybe we should buy them."

Wilma (being coy): "Well, not unless we are getting married."

Me: "I guess we shouldn't then?"

Wilma (joking, I think): "I might find my Prince Charming overseas."

After we saw Wilma off on the plane, her parents and I returned (with encouragement from Frances) to the store and I bought three heavy boxes of fine china to store in my bachelor pad.

~ Big Deal ~

Anita was planning to go to Toronto (at age 14) to study Music Theory at the Toronto Royal Conservatory.

Wilma: "How will you manage to get along all on your own in a strange big city?"

Anita: "I've been in Paris, London and New York all in one day. I think I can handle Toronto for the summer."

***

~ Research is Important ~

Wilma, talking to one of her friends in Winnipeg, said (of me): "He's a nice enough person, but not much of a kisser."

Friend (smiling broadly): "Oh. I wouldn't say that."

Wilma was furious, for reasons she didn't want to admit.

***

~It Never Hurts To Ask ~

Wilma on the phone to me: "I'm wondering if I should come home sooner than we had planned?"

Me: "It's up to you. I'll be glad to see you whenever you get here."

Wilma: "I could cancel my last tour if you wanted."

Me: "Don't come home early on my account."

She didn't, but she wasn't pleased with me.

***

On another occasion, with a different friend, Wilma told one of her Winnipeg friends that she was getting married to me.

Friend: "You mean you are marrying that rabble rouser?"

Wilma didn't find out until much later just what her friend meant.

Los Angeles January 2008
`(I'm the one without a hat)`

Wilma and I were visiting our friends, Kaori and Joel, in Los Angeles during the Writers' Guild strike. The temptation was too much for me. I had to take a bit of time for a chat and to walk the picket line.

*

***

~ Found Out ~

My son, Ken, sitting down to write his final 2nd-year Math exam at Waterloo University, looks up to a professor supervising nearby.

"Excuse me. Do you know who is the professor for this course?" he asks.

Professor: "Yes. I am."

Ken: "Oh . . . And what is your name, please?"

Ken was awarded the gold medal for excellence in Math. Not so much for class attendance.

I wonder if there is a DNA marker for this trait.

Other University Experiences

<u>University of Manitoba</u>

I have dealt with most of the important events at the U of M in previous sections because I attended there on several occasions. These are a few different stories.

*

I've never been a person to play 'practical jokes', although I must admit that I was often amused seeing other students playing them. In one Physics class the professor 'taught' the lesson by opening his folder of notes to where he had left off and then continuing to copy the notes on the blackboard until the end of the class. One day, while the professor was copying notes, one student had been set up to call the professor to the door while another student ran up to the podium, picked up a few pages, turned them over and then put them back on top of the pile.

We thought he would notice that the top page did not continue on from where he had left off and would have to find his place. The joke was on us. He just carried on copying the notes without noticing that the last sentence on the board did not lead into the next one from the notes. The next day the notes suffered another big jump in continuity when he reached the end of the reversed notes, but he just carried on with them.

I can only hope he actually noticed our trick and turned it back on us by pretending not to notice, thus leaving us with the task of having to sort out our confused notes. I'd hate to think that the notes remained out of order until he retired.

*

I tried to take an Education course in 1976 to meet an arbitrary requirement for my position as Special Education Coordinator. It was 21 years after receiving my degree in 1955. I arranged an interview with an advisor and was given a time and place to meet with her during the evening registration process. Well in advance of my appointed time, I dutifully arrived at the building specified. It appeared to be in total darkness. I tried a door. It was open so I went in, wandered around and detected a tiny gleam of light at the end of dark corridor. I knocked on the door. No answer. I knocked harder and pushed the door open a little bit, and announced myself.

"Hello. Come in." The voice seemed to come from the dark outline of a lady sitting at the desk.

"I have an appointment with you about taking a course," I suggested.

"I know. But I don't think I can help you."

"Oh," I responded as I left to find my way back down the long dark hall. I was relieved not to have to talk to her—she was scary.

Back at the lines for registration, there was a long line for former students and another one for new students. I took a wild guess and stood in the one for former students. After maybe 20 minutes in line I got a chance to hand my information to a person.

She looked at it briefly and said, " No. You haven't been a student recently. You should be in that other line."

"Yes, but I am a graduate. Doesn't that make me a former student?"

"No."

After a wait in the specified other line, I got a chance to say, "I was told I should be in this line."

"You went to university here didn't you?"

"Yes, but the lady over there said I should be this line because that was a long time ago."

"You are a former student, not a new student. You need to be in that other line."

I went back to the first line I had been in, and got to talk to the same lady again, "I tried the other line and she said I should be in this line."

"Well, I can't help you. You need to register as a new student and that is in the other line."

I started to walk back to get into the other line for another run at it, with my sheaf of papers in my hand. I stopped when I realized that I had by now spent more than an hour and a half here and was exactly at the same place as I had been when I first walked in. I'm good at Math, and a quick mental calculation told me that at this rate it would require . . . uh . . . let me see. Oh, yes. *Forever.*

I did the only thing that made sense to me at the time. I stood in the middle of the floor, tore my sheaf of accumulated pages in half and then in half again and threw them into the air high above my head as I shouted, '*aaaaagggggghhhhhh*' as loudly as I could while walking out the door.

I got in my car and drove home. The next day I told the Assistant Superintendent it was not possible for me to take that course and if I needed it for my current position then I would have to resign.

His response was short and to the point. "We can't have that. I'll call the Department of Education and tell them you don't need the course."

I'm not sure exactly what I learned from this experience, but I'm sure there is a lesson in there somewhere. By a quirk of fate, a few years later I was hired by Brandon University to teach that exact same course that I hadn't taken.

*

When my son, Ken, was in elementary grades (age 10) he was learning computer programming. There were no PC, Radio Shack, or Apple computers at that time. I taught computer science using pencil mark IBM cards, which required an oval to be filled in for each character. It was slow work and then they would have to be mailed away for the cards to be read and processed, making a time delay of about a week. There was also a problem if even a single oval was coded incorrectly. Computers require perfection, so the pack of cards would have to be returned, corrected, and then the whole batch sent back again for another try at running the program—another week delay.

I made arrangements with the University of Manitoba to have Ken use their computer lab to get a more effective experience. On one occasion he was there at a terminal programming furiously, while I sat at a table reading, when the woman supervising the room noticed him.

"He will have to leave. We don't allow children to play with our computers," she said to me.

"He isn't playing. He is programming with APL (a computer language for handling arrays)," I responded. "Just have a look and see what he is doing."

She declined my offer to look at the computer screen and said, "Whose account is he using?"

"Mine. But I only got the account so he could use the computers. I have a card here from the director of Computer Science authorizing him to use the lab," I suggested, showing her the card.

"If it is your account then you have to use the terminal and he can sit at the table."

"I don't even know how to program APL."

"He will have to sit at the table. You sit at the terminal."

I left Ken at the table, went to the Engineering Building, up to the seventh floor and knocked on the door of the director. Very apologetically, I explained the situation and asked him if he could phone the computer lab and explain to the woman that Ken was authorized to use the terminal.

I went back to the computer lab. Ken continued working at his APL programming while I sat at the table reading my book. The woman periodically looked over to glare at us until we left.

I should mention it was refreshing that at both at the University of Winnipeg and the University of Manitoba the professors talked directly to Ken at their level of communication rather than talking down to him because of his size or age. Not many adults did.

*

In 1962, the Shell Oil Company awarded me one of their 'Shell Merit Fellowships' to attend a special program for Science teachers through the auspices of the Leland Stanford Junior University in Palo Alto, California. They awarded only one fellowship per province and paid all expenses, so needless to say, I was delighted to have the opportunity. When I registered and found out the cost of the fees they were covering I was even more delighted.

Initially, I wondered why they called it a 'Junior University'. That gives you some idea as to how naïve I was in those days—obviously, it was named after Leland Stanford Junior.

The program was on the cutting edge of new developments in several fields of science, with cost being of no consideration. For example, a prominent Mathematician, Dr. G. Polya, was brought from overseas just to teach the ten of us one course. I never missed any of his classes in spite of the area around the lecture hall being rife with allergy producing plants. I would end up with several soggy handkerchiefs by the end of every class, but it was worth it.

His favorite question as he worked through a Math problem was, "Now, do you believe it more, or do you believe it less?"

Most Math teachers would say, "Is it right or is it wrong?"

When we filled out a form at the end of the program, most of the class filled in his name as the most memorable part of the program.

*

One of our class members was a Catholic priest. He had a car (an old wreck, actually) and liked seeing the sights of the area but didn't like driving. I acted as his driver on occasion for tours of San Francisco. When the program ended and we were planning how we would get back to our respective homes, he let it be known that he would appreciate company (i.e., a driver) for the drive to Seattle, Washington, because it was hosting the Century 21 Exposition World Fair. It was sort of on my way home (more north than east, but close enough) and would save me a bit on the cost of my bus ticket. So I took a deep breath (I always had serious doubts that the car would be up to making any trip, no matter how short, successfully) and agreed.

On the day we left, he pulled out a small bottle of water, walked around the car carefully sprinkling each fender, and said a few words. We had no trouble on the drive. There have been numerous times afterwards that I regretted not asking him for some of that water.

But then again, maybe it was only effective when he said the pertinent words.

*

University of North Dakota (1967)

I learned a lot of things by getting my master's degree from the University of North Dakota (UND) Most of them had nothing to do directly with the actual classes or program.

*

It started when I met my faculty advisor to set up courses and things like that. I suggested I wanted to finish the program in one year because Wilma was expecting our first child.

"I'm sorry. It is a two-year program," she said.

"Who do I see so I can do it in one year?" I asked.

"You could go see the registrar, but it is a two-year course."

I went to the registrar's office and said to the girl at the reception desk, "I want to take my master's degree program in one year."

"It's a two-year program."

"I know. Who should I see in order to do it in one year? "

She gave me the name of person to see.

I saw the man and he said, "You can try if you want, but it will be hard work."

I assured him I had nothing else to do with my time. Back I went to my advisor to have my selection of courses approved.

"I see you have opted to take psychology. Your program is in education. You'd never pass that psychology course. It is for people enrolled in psychology, not education."

"Is there any reason I can't take it? Other than that I might fail it?"

"No. But you'll never pass it."

I did take it and passed it. I even got the highest mark in the class on one test. Neither the psychology professor nor his regular psychology students liked that at all.

*

I did have some inconveniences in organizing my program to fit my half-courses together. I had to take some 'advanced' courses in the first semester and then the 'introductory' courses the second semester. It really didn't seem to make much difference.

*

For amusement, I started a non-paying job as research assistant for one of my professors. His project looked interesting and I thought I could use some experience in educational research. He had done a first run of correlating the data from his randomly selected sample with his hypothesis. What he wanted me to do was to go through his sample and remove all the subjects who didn't correlate the way he wanted.

When I questioned him as to how he would justify this, his answer was, "Obviously they are not typical members of the sample and should be removed."

At this point I apologetically excused myself from the project with the excuse I was finding myself too busy with my course work. I'm sure he and others have found computers to be useful tools in finding irregular subjects to be removed from their sample group and hence obtain a more suitable correlation.

*

Two things I learned from another student's counseling practicum experience:

1) If you are going to make sexual advances and proposition a high school student whom you are counseling, remember to turn off the tape recorder.

2) If you forget to turn off the recorder and record your conversation with her, then do not play that tape to be critiqued by your faculty advisor.

Otherwise, he won't pass you.

*

One of the psychology majors in my class did not like it when I would sometimes displace him as the one getting the highest mark on a psychology test because I was just a lowly education major.

One day he approached me and said: "James isn't going to be able to take the test tomorrow because he is ill. Everyone is going to stay away from the test so his being absent won't penalize him. Can we count on you to stay away?"

I replied, "Sure, if everyone else does."

Ten minutes after the time scheduled for the start of the test, I decided to stroll down the hall past the testing room. I wasn't surprised to see everyone except me, including James, busily sitting there working on the test.

I walked in, sat down, wrote the test, and got a higher mark than he did. That time, the professor neglected to announce who got the highest mark until a student prompted him.

I never said anything to the fellow about it, but I did give him a knowing look and tiny nod every time I happened to catch his eye.

He and I never became good friends.

*

My experiences continued on into writing my thesis. It began with my advisor not liking my thesis topic. He said it wasn't firmly based on someone else's previous research. As in, I was supposed to do research to provide support for previously written research. I, as usually naïve, had thought my original idea would be more useful. After a short and one-sided discussion I agreed to change from originality to an analysis of a questionnaire based on a questionnaire someone else had done. At least I got to modify it.

The title was impressive, 'The Preferred and Actual Practices of Guidance Counsellors in the Public Schools of Manitoba'. But already I was in trouble. I was in the United States where they spell it as 'counselor', with one 'l', not two.

The people to whom I would be giving the questionnaire were Canadian and would expect two while the university wanted one. That problem was resolved after much frustration, discussion, explanation, and checking of the manuscript as to whom it was referring and who would be reading it.

All went well. I typed up the thesis, got signatures of all the advisors, etc., and submitted it. I returned to Portage to help Wilma await the arrival of our first baby. Then I got a phone call. I needed to return to Grand Forks to correct a 'spelling error' in the manuscript. When I got the manuscript, I discovered that the error was on the signature page ('hte' instead of 'the'). I was told I had to retype the page because a correction could not be allowed on the signature page. This was in the days before computers and everything had to be typed manually . . . and on the same typewriter. I found the typewriter I had used originally, got the advisor signatures (one professor was at a party), and handed it to the secretary at the Dean's Office for his signature.

I sat down to wait. After maybe 10 minutes she came back and said that this being Friday afternoon I would have to come back on Monday because the Dean didn't have time to sign it right now. While I had been waiting in the anteroom I couldn't help but overhear the Dean talking on the phone arranging to play golf in about 30 minutes. This tidbit of information led me to question her plan.

"Can't he sign it now? I live in Canada and I need to get home because my wife is the hospital having our first baby," I said. "I told her I'd be there to visit her tonight."

"Sorry. You will have to come back on Monday," she said.

"Oh. Well, if that's the case, there's no problem. When you come in on Monday, you'll find me sitting right here."

I sat firmly down on a chair, with the comment, "Right here."

"You are not planning to stay here all weekend?" she asked, with a surprised look on her face.

"I have nothing else to do."

"I'm sorry. We can't allow you to stay here overnight."

"Then you can call the police and have me arrested. At least then I'll have a free room. And they will probably feed me, too."

At this point, she beat a hasty retreat into the back room where the Dean clearly would have heard the verbal exchange. Two minutes later she came out and handed me my copy of my signed thesis. Right behind her was the Dean with his golf clubs over his shoulder. He beat me out the door.

I went home to be there when my darling baby, Ken, arrived.

*

University of Waterloo (1976)

Maybe I shouldn't include the University of Waterloo here; the only time I set foot on the campus was for my son Ken's graduation. I do have very good feelings about the university because it helped get Ken on his way into the field of Computer Science.

He was in Grade 4 and interested in computers. I happened to see an advertisement from the University of Waterloo promoting correspondence courses, one of which was computer science. I promptly sent in his application (he was only 10 years old . . . so?). I got a reply accepting him with the condition he would need to show credit in Grade 12 Mathematics. The obvious (to me) solution was for me to register for the course and he could do it. So we did.

A problem arose when it became clear that he would have to pass the midterm exam in order to get the second half of the course. There would be no problem in his passing the course. There was a problem in that the course was registered in my name and it would be violation of everything teachers hold sacred for me to have someone else write my exam for me . . . no matter how old he might be.

Well, I've never met a problem I can't solve—maybe not well, but I can solve it. I would have to write the exam. It was registered in my name so that would be simple enough. Oh, yes, one minor glitch. I didn't know anything about computer programming. I had a few weeks, so it should be easy enough.

It wasn't. There were several nights after 8:30 (Ken's bedtime) as I worked on the course while Ken was sound asleep in his bed that I would get stuck on something.

I would sneak quietly up to his room and whisper something in his ear like, "Ken . . . how do you do 'read data statements'?"

Without rousing or opening his eyes, Ken would give a concise explanation. I would return to my assignment.

I got a reasonable passing mark on the midterm and Ken got to finish the course. Because I've always had a compulsion about closure, I also wrote the final exam and passed, giving me a credit in Computer Science 101. It later was useful for me to know how to program and Ken had the fun of doing the course.

This was obviously a classic case of, 'It isn't where you're going—it's how you get there'.

*

University of the State of New York - (1977)

I had read somewhere that degrees in the State of New York are all issued by the state, based on courses taken and grades assigned by separate universities scattered throughout the state, and in some cases, outside the state.

My penchant for taking random university courses had resulted in my having more than a dozen course credits that had not been used anywhere as credit for a degree. My overactive brain put the two facts together and came up with an idea. Maybe the State of New York would accept my Canadian and U.S. courses for credit toward a degree. I gathered up mark statements from all my universities (except Waterloo—I didn't feel right about using it as a credit) and submitted them to the University of the State of New York. I expected I would have to take a few courses to make up the credit distribution required, but they checked the courses, asked a few questions about them, and issued me a Bachelor of Arts degree in Liberal Studies.

I submitted my new degree to the Manitoba Department of Education and they moved me up one level in my salary category. I had never set foot in the University of the State of New York, but then, neither had any of their other graduates.

*

University of Connecticut (Storrs) - (1986)

I was appointed Coordinator for Gifted Students in the Portage School Division with a mandate to follow the model established by Dr. Joseph Renzulli at the university in Storrs, Connecticut. This seemed like a good opportunity to add another university to my arsenal, so I spent my summer holidays at Confratute 1986 under the personal direction of Renzulli and a cast of hundreds (literally). The rather strange name—and one I have always found strangely disturbing—is accurately described on their website as:

" . . . conceived as a combination of the best aspects of a **Con**ference, and an insti**tute** with a good deal of **fra**ternity blended within."

It is a high-power, intense smorgasbord of courses, activities, and demonstrations by classes of gifted students from the region. Renzulli's model encourages teachers and parents to have gifted students work on *real-life* activities and projects with displays or presentations for a *real* audience—outside the classroom walls or preferably outside the school walls.

It still runs every year and I highly recommend it for anyone who is looking for an exhausting but exhilarating summer experience. It would be just as good for parents as it is for teachers.

I notice (courtesy of Google) that they are presently setting up for Confratute 2009 . . . their 31st year of them.

***

~ Helpful ~

We were living in a basement suite in Grand Forks and had bought a new barbecue with rotisserie. We were using it for the first time to roast a small chicken. We left the chicken slowly rotating over the bed of hot coals while we went shopping. When we returned, the landlady came out to meet us.

"I saw you had left the barbecue running and I was afraid the chicken would burn. So I unplugged it," she said.

We looked at our poor little chicken that had been cooking without rotating. Fortunately, it had stopped with its back toward the coals. We did manage to make a meal from the front of it.

***

~ The Joys Of True And False ~

The psychology professor had us marking our true/false exam questions. I was doing quite well until I noticed one of his answers was different from mine.

On checking the question, I noticed it had a double negative in the statement, making my answer right and his answer wrong.

Since he frequently reused exams and tests, I felt I should point out to him why his answer was wrong.

He made a wry face, and said, "You can't tell me you noticed that when you answered the question."

So I didn't try to tell him that it was obvious to me—because I don't never use no double negatives.

MY TR3—THROUGH THE DECADES

My carefree bachelor days 1960

Portage Collegiate parade 1980 (Ken & Anita)

The 3rd generation 2008 Lillian and Emma

Some Counseling Events

For my master's degree I had taken courses in psychotherapy and took advantage of opportunities to augment my skills in various techniques after graduation. I had many chances to make use of these skills. These are just a few of them.

*

One Monday morning, at 9:15 I had a highly agitated student appear at my door. He had gone to class thinking he was finished with his weekend LSD trip but, after sitting in class for a few minutes, he was upset by his perception that the classroom walls were changing shape and moving around in a most disturbing manner and threatened to crush him. My plan was just to be reassuring and let time pass until the effect of the drug wore off.

He said he needed a smoke and I said it was alright. Even though smoking in the office was not officially authorized, I did permit it when I felt circumstances warranted it. Then he asked for a match. I didn't have one so I went to the staff room and asked for one. One of the teachers offered me one of the six-inch-long book of paper matches that were popular for advertising at that time.

I couldn't very well tell them why that would make my client freak out. That left me babbling incoherently until another teacher gave me a regular size matchbook.

*

She was a student from the other high school. I had counselled her previously as a potential suicide, and from her demeanour I knew why

162

she wanted to see me. I guided her from the anteroom into my private office at which time she shoved a handful of pills into her mouth, presumably to swallow them.

She hadn't counted on my having been a farm boy who had experience with forcing a sheep or cow's mouth open to slip in a pill or two. The process was just the opposite for her. Before she could swallow I grabbed her throat, squeezed her cheeks to open her mouth, and the pills spewed out on the floor. She was surprisingly strong, but I forced each of her hands open and more pills hit the floor. I scooped up the pills and put them in my pocket.

I had no way of knowing whether or not she had swallowed pills previously, but from her drugged appearance I felt she had. I left her in the relative safety of my office and went out to the anteroom. Two male students were putting in time looking the pamphlets on display there.

I went over to them, and said, "I need you to do something. There is a girl in my office and you have to keep her from leaving."

They looked at me a bit vacantly, and muttered, "What? Why?"

"Just do it. Use physical force if you have to, but don't let her out the door. It is very important. I'll be back right away."

I jogged to the office and told the principal to call an ambulance immediately. While he was dialing, I gave him a quick run down and then jogged back the guidance office.

The girl was still in my office and the two worried students in the anteroom were still standing there wondering what was going on. I thanked them profusely for their help, which confused them even more because they hadn't done anything, but they were relieved to be off duty and fled the area.

The ambulance arrived at a side door and the girl was hustled to the hospital to get her stomach pumped. I phoned her parents and went back to my regular day's work.

*

I had been counselling the student on a regular weekly basis concerning his negative feelings about his family.

Student: "I miss my father."

Me (being a totally Rogerian counselor): "You miss your father?"

Student: "I didn't even get to go to his funeral."

Me: "You wish you could have gone to his funeral?"

Student: "Yes."

You may have noticed that the Rogerian method uses a technique of rephrasing the student's statements and feeding them back to him for elaboration. It looks totally lame in print, but does work well in many actual situations.

His 'Yes' response didn't give me much to work on. If I asked him 'Why' it probably wouldn't elicit much more than some superficial answer.

So I took a shot in the dark. "How would that have made a difference to you?"

Student: "I have a lot of things I wanted to tell him, but now I never can."

Me (being Rogerian again): "You feel you need to get some things off your chest to him?"

Student: "Yes."

Me: "Are you willing to try something which might help?"

Student: "Yes."

At this point I took a deep breath and set the Rogerian method aside. I tried a technique I had seen demonstrated but had never tried it. I set an empty chair in the middle of the room with the student sitting facing it. I sat off to the side and a bit behind the student so I was out of his range of vision.

We did some deep relaxation exercises (close eyes, relax, concentrate on being aware of parts of his body, etc.). Then, with his eyes closed, I had him visualize his father sitting in the chair and told him to open his eyes when he was ready to talk to his father.

In most of the demonstrations I had seen, the facilitator would stand behind the empty chair and provide responses as if they were from the person in the empty chair as necessary to keep the process moving along. In this case he knew what he wanted to say and he did for most of an hour. My only role was simply to provide a few supportive, encouraging comments.

The student told me afterwards that it had seemed totally real and he felt a lot better. It was an amazingly successful session.

*

The phone rang about midnight and roused me out of a sound sleep. A young voice on the phone said something like, "Our friend needs your help. Can you meet him on the lawn by the School Division Office?"

"Yes. Tell him I will be there in fifteen minutes."

I parked my car in the parking lot and wandered onto the lawn area with no one in sight in the darkened area. At moments like this it never occurred to me that someone might just be playing a joke on me. In all my years, no one ever set me up with a late night call. I guess they had better things to do late at night.

A slight, young fellow walked out from among the trees, walked toward me and we met in the middle of the lawn. To anyone looking at us they could easily assume it was a drug deal or something even more nefarious. We each introduced ourselves to the other by first name only and walked over to my car without further words.

We drove around, ate a couple of snacks and drank coffee. He said he wasn't on drugs and I believed him. But he was severely depressed. About 2 AM he gave me permission to call his parents to let them know he was alright, in case they were worried about him. I had a very short conversation with his dad who advised me that they were glad he ran away, and no, they did not want me to bring him home then or any time in the future. That didn't leave me with very many options.

I decided I would take him home with me—that's what I would have done with a lost puppy. Wilma was accepting, as always, of our having a houseguest about whom we knew nothing, except that I considered him to be potentially suicidal.

He asked if he could have a bath. I got him soap and a towel and he went into the bathroom. I heard the water running to fill the tub … and running … and still running. I was getting worried because I knew a bathtub of water was useful for a successful suicide by keeping a slit wrist from healing over. I tried the door and it was locked. Wilma and I discussed the various scenarios—that he had killed himself with the water running was near the top of the list.

I knew how to unlock it with a paperclip, but I wasn't sure I wanted to burst into the bathroom to confront a naked teenager with my lack of trust in him. I couldn't think of a good opening line, so I waited a bit longer. At last the water flow stopped.

Eventually, he came out and we put him up on a hide-a-bed in the basement for the night.

The next day, I took him home for some highly directive counseling with him and his parents.

The parents called me back on two occasions later for booster talks. At least that way I didn't have to lose sleep.

*

I used to do weight lifting off and on for most of my younger years and had a set of barbells in the basement.

We had just taken in an aboriginal (First Nation) youth as a temporary 'foster' placement. It was suppertime and he wasn't responding to my calling down the stairs.

When I went down, I found him lying on the floor with the bar resting solidly across his neck, fortunately being supported by the large diameter 25 lb weights on each end pinning him to the floor. If they had been smaller diameter weights it might easily have choked him.

I offered to teach him a bit about weight lifting, but he seemed to have lost his enthusiasm for it.

*

One of the local agencies, I don't remember which one—I frequently got referrals from several of them— phoned me and asked if I could visit a young native (First Nation) lady whom they thought was suicidal.

She opened the door. I introduced myself and said who had sent me.

"Tea?" she asked.

"Yes. Thank you."

I sat at the table facing a clock on the wall. In my readings about First Nation peoples I had learned they prefer silence to idle chatter.

Like most white men, I felt the need to fill any silence with words. She made the tea and we sat opposite each other sipping tea in silence.

I strengthened my resolve to be silent by thinking, "I'll wait for thirty minutes for her to make the first conversational gambit."

We sat sipping tea while I watched the slow progress of the clock. It was close to twenty minutes of silence before she spoke. After she told me the problem, it was easily resolved.

Her husband was getting out of jail soon and in spite of a restraining order (which she didn't fully understand) he had said he would be arriving on her doorstep. It had been an abusive relationship and she was scared.

Finding a temporary place for her to stay proved to be a much better solution than suicide—the only alternative she thought she had.

*

I have always been interested in ideas like levitation and psychic experiences. In selected classes and small group sessions I used relaxation activities the get students into a relaxed mood. They would be told to lie down with eyes closed and then to concentrate sequentially on selected specific parts of their body. I would instruct them something like this:

"Concentrate on your left foot. Imagine you are your big toe and feel the pressure of your shoe and the other toes on it. Feel how warm and stuffy it is there. Now concentrate on the pressure of your head on the flour."

The relaxation was always successful. So successful, in fact, that I moved it up a level. I would have the students mentally examine their face details, and then imagine they were rising out of their body and looking down at themselves. While they were looking down at themselves on the floor I would encourage them to talk to themselves. It was surprising that most of them actually felt they were looking down at themselves on the floor. A few of them—mostly ones with problems— felt they benefited from hearing what they had to say to themselves.

*

Somewhat related to the above activity is a useless, but interesting, party activity I did several times. One person (me) would sit in a chair. Four students would clasp their hands together with two fingers extended, and then lift me off the chair using only their fingers under my arms and knees. Usually they would not succeed at all. Sometimes they would struggle and manage to tip me a bit, but never get me off the chair.

They would then put all their hands on top of each other on my head and push down for about fifteen seconds. They would then try to lift me in the same way as before. Invariably, they could lift me easily and in a few cases to their shoulder height— high enough to scare me.

It seemed to work best when I was the person being lifted. Probably this was because I would think 'heavy' when they were pushing my head downwards and think 'light' when they started to lift me.

My normal weight divided by four was at least forty pounds (18 kilograms).

***

~ The Moment of Decision ~

Sitting in my car in front of the 7-Eleven with a suicidal student after driving around for hours talking.

Student: "I need a cigarette."

Me: "No problem. I'll get you one."

Me: " Should I buy a pack? I'm sure I must know someone in there who would give me one or two cigarettes. I don't smoke (which was not exactly true). If I buy a pack and you kill yourself tonight – the rest will just be wasted."

Student (after thinking in silence for a couple of minutes): "Buy a pack."

Me: "Are you sure?"

Student: (after another long pause): "Yeah."

I bought a LARGE pack.

***

~ He Should Have A Driver's License ~

Lady on the telephone, after telling me how she teleports herself to relatives all over Canada to visit them on weekends:

"How old should my son be before I allow him to teleport himself outside the city?"

Me: "How old is he now?"

Lady: "Fourteen."

Me: "Eighteen. He should be an adult before he makes choices like that."

And then I explained why he shouldn't travel anywhere alone until he was sixteen, even by car.

***

~ I Lose—I Win ~

Portage was a small city. But we did have frequently gang wars and student harassment by gangs. Girl gangs were the toughest and most ruthless, but that is another story.

Me (to Steve, leader of a junior high gang): "You want to arm wrestle?"

Steve (showing off to the rest of the class watching): "Sure. I can take anyone."

We went at it. He was good, but I knew I could take him whenever I wanted. I looked him in the eye, and pushed him a bit, and then let up. He knew.

We had a non-verbal conversation, loosely translated as follows:

Steve's eyes said: "I gotta win. I'm the leader. If I lose this, I lose everything."

My eyes replied: "OK. Just for you. But don't forget it."

And I let him win . . . after putting up a good fight.

The gang never caused any problems in my school again.

***

- Food For Thought -

Wilma to our son-in-law, Henry: "I learned from my dad not to believe anything I was told and only half of what I see."
Henry: " Did he tell you that or show you?"

Baby Dog
Aug 11, 1991 - May 8, 2007

Joe . . . My 17-Year Counselling Session

The background for this story begins with my search for some meaningful way of changing the lives for people who were caught in an unsuccessful life or in malfunctioning homes, environments or relationships.

I became involved in several of the sensitivity group programs that were popular at the time in hopes they would provide me with some clues. They did seem to increase the level of connection and acceptance present within a group of strangers. However, the feelings of safety and openness within the sensitivity group did not seem to be very useful, or even acceptable, with other people who had not gone through the process. In many ways, a Caribbean cruise is similar to a residential sensitivity group, except that the people on a cruise can escape from each other if they want.

I also had some unresolved thoughts after watching a National Film Board documentary about the experiences of a person (later to became the mayor of Winnipeg) who had befriended a teenager and tried (unsuccessfully) for a couple of years to integrate him into society. He gave it a good try, and at times appeared to be making progress, but it ended unsuccessfully. I felt he could have succeeded if only he hadn't given up so soon.

Having spent a lot of my life observing children in undesirable home situations, or in unsuitable school classrooms, I realized there is a theory that provides a beginning point in understand how to help them. My extension of the psychological theory of 'cognitive dissonance' is that a person will become progressively more uncomfortable living in an environment that does not match his.

Suppose a generally good person is put him in jail. The 'bad' prison environment implies to him that he must be a 'bad' person because he is there and he begins to accept this as his self-image. This new self-image creates dissonance between his previous 'good person' self-image and his 'bad' environment. In order to reduce this dissonance he can:

(a) Accept that he is a 'bad' person and change his thoughts and actions to become a 'bad' person, or

(b) He may try to change the environment by helping other prisoners and improving conditions, or change his perception of it by rationalizing his views of prison (it's not as bad as expected, I can take courses here, etc.) to believe it is 'good.'

In any case, he will think and act in some manner to reconcile his self-image with his environment.

Children's Aid organizations take children from bad living environments and place them into a more acceptable environment. They hope that the child will feel an inner discomfort with misbehaving in the supportive environment and will change to match the environment as a way of reducing the inner stress. I have seen occasional cases where the child's ego is strong enough to alter the environment to justify his misbehaviors.

It is a rule of thumb in integrating children with behavioral problems into a regular class that you need a ratio of not more than 1 in 10. Otherwise, there is a real danger that the regular children will pick up the undesirable characteristics rather than the other way around. The undesirable behaviors are much more obvious and hence can easily be perceived as a major part of the environment.

I could have said all that in a much simpler manner—people will try to 'fit in'. However, that isn't always true—in some cases they will try to make their environment 'fit in' with their own low self-image. And therein lies the challenge.

Enter Joe into my life. He was eighteen-years-old when I met him. He was living on his own, having left his remarried mother and their dysfunctional and disruptive home several years earlier.

I met Joe by accident while he was attending Grade 12 in Winnipeg at Sturgeon Creek Collegiate. He and a girl shared the rent in a rather rundown apartment. He invited me to his apartment so we could talk about volunteers for the upcoming Fringe Festival—a yearly summer event in Winnipeg of short plays written and performed by amateurs.

I sat on the sofa. It seemed to have no springs, and I sank into it up to my armpits, or so it seemed. He watched to see my reaction and I tried to pretend this was a normal thing for me. He told me later he got it for ten dollars from one of the other tenants. I think he paid too much for it.

We were talking when he got a phone call. I couldn't help overhearing his side of the conversation (from his mother, as I later learned). To him, it seemed to be an everyday conversation with his mother. He spoke in a calm unemotional manner, but what he said shocked me.

"Maybe you've forgiven him for raping my sister, but I'm not having him come here to live here with me," he said into the phone.

I had some trouble getting my mind around what he had said. It didn't help much when I learned the person they were talking about was his stepfather.

The counselor/psychologist in me pricked up its ears. This could be interesting person to get to know. He was obviously a person with a strong ego (I was later to learn just how strong his ego really is). It seems he had been involved in a less than ideal home environment from the moment he was born. His mother insisted on holding him and keeping him briefly after he was born—just long enough for any bonding or imprinting to take place—before giving him up for adoption.

Then she decided she should take him and go to live with his grandmother, instead of adoption. After that, he went to an aunt for two months, and then to grandparents for several months before going to Winnipeg with his mother. After that he bounced around a lot—back to his aunt, at group homes, his ex-girlfriend's parents, all including intervals with his mother and his stepfather.

When I met Joe, he was struggling financially—he had just discovered that 'rent-to-own' still meant you needed money to pay money to pay the rent with interest— and emotionally. He had re-entered school in order to get his Grade 12. He seemed to have an inner need to make his life into something more than it was, which wasn't setting the bar very high.

After knowing Joe for a few weeks, I got the idea that he would be a perfect person to try out my ideas about how a person can be encouraged to change himself by putting him into an environment that would be in conflict with his current life and self-image (as a hopeless loser). I suggested to him that I would like to help him improve his life. His response was that he was going to adopt me. I thought he was kidding. He wasn't. He still sends me Father's Day cards and we still exchange daily emails after some seventeen years.

I agreed to help him, and be a surrogate father, on condition that I would not be involved in any way with his mother, fathers (real and step), brothers and sisters. I knew that if I got involved with seven additional people like him, I would be the one to change and become like them, instead of his becoming a useful member of society like me.

My initial plan was to get him out of the apartment which he shared with a strange girl (I think anyone who punches holes in her house mate's water bed when he is away is strange) and however many mice lived in the hole at floor level in the living room wall. He was getting social assistance payments as a high school student. A cynical person might think that he was in school just to get the money. I didn't.

He moved into an adequately nice high-rise (top floor, of course, for the view). His mother promptly convinced him to have his younger brother come to live with him. It did help him with the higher rent.

One day, shortly after Joe and his brother got settled into the new apartment, I got a phone call from Joe.

"I'm going to buy a puppy."

I responded with, "You can't afford a puppy."

"She's had all her shots and everything. And I can make money selling her pups."

"How much would she cost?" I asked.

"Only $450, and I can get her with really small payments."

I decided to play tough:

"You can't afford payments on a dog. You don't have any spare money. Besides, you'll never be around to look after her. This is totally crazy."

"She's in the mall pet shop. You should go and see her. Her name is Baby."

I took one last desperate shot before I hung up, "If you buy that dog I'll never talk to you again."

A few days later, I went to the pet shop, just out of curiosity. There was an empty cage in the dog section. On the outside of the cage were the handwritten words, "Her name is Baby."

The next time I went to see Joe, I was met at the door by a tiny bundle of fur twirling around and around on the floor. I picked her up and she licked my ear. I just knew she loved me—until I noticed she did that for everyone coming into the apartment.

A year later, Baby suffered a broken leg after Joe had moved to Edmonton leaving his brother with her in the apartment. When I brought Baby to Joe's apartment from the veterinarian, Joe's brother didn't answer the doorbell. We waited around, assuming he was out, and eventually ended up bringing Baby (complete with leg splint) home with me.

It was supposed to be just until her leg healed, but she stayed with us for the next 15 years. Up until that time, neither Wilma nor I would have qualified for the term, 'pet people'.

Dr. Peter looked after Baby's broken leg and then some ten years later tried to fix her deteriorating leg joints. He went well beyond the call of his profession in taking X-rays, consulting with specialists and suggesting supplements like Glucosamine. He even suggested that buying it at Safeway was cheaper than from him. Her legs were a real challenge for him because they were so tiny, but he never gave up.

I have been a significant part of Joe's life (and he of mine) for some seventeen years. We have been crazy angry at each many times, but somehow we are kindred spirits. Although we are at least a generation apart in age and from different backgrounds, we had experienced similar traumas growing up. This background meant that we understood each other on a level that didn't require words. We may not always appear to be friends in the usual meaning of the word, but are always there for each other when the situation requires it—no matter what.

I don't want to go into details here because he wants me to write his biography someday and I don't want to give away all the surprises. So far, all I have is a tentative title, 'Life Is Not a Gay Bar'.

Joe made a lot of false starts, but he has obtained his Grade 12, completed courses in film production and in office/business operation. For over two years, he owned and operated a small upscale, modern clothing store in Winnipeg—not the best market in the world because Winnipeg is not a city noted for high living and first-class spending. He has worked for talent agencies in Vancouver and is presently running a food preparation and delivery service for selected businesses in Vancouver.

Currently he is in professional therapy to help him cope with some of the problems created by his childhood and youth. It has been a seventeen-year trip, with a lot of ups and downs, but Joe is now a relatively successful, working, tax-paying member of society. He even budgets and tries to plan ahead—emphasis on the word 'tries'.

He has changed both himself and his environment several times and in many ways, and is beginning to feel comfortable with his new life.

He may still be a work in progress, but the progress so far is impressive. Although he won't admit it yet, he really doesn't need me any more . . . except as a friend.

***

~ Talk About Stubborn ~

Joe and I were shopping for some weight equipment and kitchen utensils at The Bay. They were on different floors. We got on the elevator.

He pushed the button for the 4th floor and I pushed the one for the 3rd floor.

Me: "The weight equipment is on the 3rd floor."

Joe: "We are going to the 4th floor first."

The elevator stopped at the 3rd floor. I got off and held the door open for him. He ignored me and the elevator went on upwards.

We passed each other moments later. I was on the up escalator and he was on the down escalator. He waited for me on the 3rd floor . . . not because he was giving in to me; it was just easier that way.

He got to stand there while I went up, crossed over, and then came down again.

***

~ Gotcha ~

Me (to Anita): "Dr. Peter told me Baby should be taking Glucosamine for her joints."

Anita: "So how do you give it to her?"

Me: "I open a capsule and pour out about a tenth of it and mix it into her food. Then I take the rest of it myself. I figure it would be good for my arthritis."

Anita (in horror): "What? You are taking the dog's medicine?"

Me: "No, silly. She takes my medicine—I buy it at Safeway."

***

~ Like Father, Like Son ~

Ken tells this story on himself.

Ken, his wife Kathryn, and his young daughter Sydney, were leaving their friend's engagement party in Santa Cruz. They encountered a group of knavish looking young people blocking their way.

Ken was familiar with my story about walking through groups like that so he decided, "If my dad can do it, we can do it."

Ken put on his most stern look and they walked right through the middle of the group without incident.

Later, Ken said to us, "I realized afterwards that I might have looked more intimidating if I hadn't been carrying Sydney's American Girl doll under my arm."

1959 TR3A 40 -YEAR FACE LIFT

Guardian Angels And Unusual Things

Ockham's Razor is a 14th Century philosophical axiom, which says, in effect, "All other things being equal, the simplest solution is the best."

There have been a few times in my life when events occurred which can be best explained by the intervention of a guardian angel or some non-natural force. Other attempts to explain them seriously fail Ockham's test.

*

The most striking example is the time my friend, Milton, and I were sitting in my Triumph drinking a couple of beers while we waited for my landlady to come home and unlock the door so we could go in. At the time, I didn't know she was, in fact, at home and had reported to the police that we were drinking in a public place—a big legal *faux pas*, particularly since Milt was underage and I was his teacher.

We each had a bottle of beer half empty when the police car pulled up directly behind us and two officers surrounded the car. At their request, we both got out of the car. I tried the standard hiding technique of shoving the bottle under my belt and buttoning my jacket over it. However, they were a smart pair, and I was immediately relieved of my bottle.

The unexplained thing is that Milt's bottle had disappeared, beer and all. He had no explanation of how or where it went, but he and I both knew he had a half-full bottle just before the police pulled up. The Triumph is an open car and the police could see everything inside as they walked up. They search him and the car. After they left, we searched the car. Milt's bottle never was found—not then, and not later.

You might think it could have just slipped under a seat or into the upholstery, but the Triumph was a Spartan car, unlike modern cars—there are no hiding places. Besides, when I repaired and painted it, it was stripped down to the bare metal—inside and out. No beer bottle.

*

Another unusual, but more possibly explainable, experience concerns the time after a birthday celebration. Wilma and I took our friend, Fran, out for a birthday dinner in Winnipeg. We met Fran at the restaurant; I ordered a half-liter of wine because none of us was a big wine drinker. When I asked for three glasses, the waitress said we would have to purchase a full liter if we were using three glasses. Under different circumstances, I might have questioned her ruling on the grounds of common sense, but this was a celebration.

We got our wine. Wilma and Fran had a glass each and I drank way more of the remainder than I should have (my Scottish ancestors made me do it). Fran drove herself home and Wilma and I headed out of Winnipeg.

Suddenly, I found we were being funneled off onto an empty lot where there were a lot of police cars. It was a 'check stop' to find drivers who had been drinking. That would be me, but there was no way out.

I stopped, rolled down my window and tried not to breathe. The policeman came over, shone his flashlight at me but ignored our little dog, Baby, sleeping peacefully on Wilma's lap.

"Good evening, sir. Have you been drinking tonight?" the policeman asked.

My brain went into overtime while the question hung in the air, like a bad smell, while he awaited my reply. It wasn't all that tough a question to answer. I just didn't care much for the consequences of my answer. Lying would have just meant I would have to take a breathalyzer test and fail it. Saying I had been drinking would have led to the same result. The penalty could have been confiscation of my car, temporarily, but still very inconvenient, and a significant fine.

While I was mulling over my lack of options, Baby jumped off Wilma's lap and onto my arm, which was resting on the open window.

Baby's face was inches from the officer's hand. She leaned out the window and licked his hand.

Now, Baby was a sweet little dog but generally just tolerated strangers. She rarely licked stranger's fingers, even when urged to do so. Her actions that night were very much out of character.

The policeman was entranced with Baby, petted her, and even called for the officers to come and see her.

My inner reaction to that idea was, "Oh, sure. Let's get some more cops in on this disaster."

The other officers declined to join our little gathering. The policeman patted Baby for a few moments and then said, "Have a good night, sir."

Wilma put Baby back on her lap and Baby went back to sleep immediately—her work was done and I didn't have to answer the policeman's question. This story may not pass a rigorous examination *à la* Ockham's razor, but I think it's a good story anyway.

*

One of my friends presented me with an unusual experience—actually several experiences but the others would make up a book all by themselves.

He was living in a basement suite in Regina. He had told me his house was haunted and I should see it. Wilma and I happened to be going through Regina on our way to somewhere west and I decided it was an offer I couldn't refuse.

I set up my visit with rigorous scientific precision. I did not allow him to tell me anything (other than his initial statement that it was haunted, and that's a pretty wide category). I had him blindfold me before I went in and guided me by voice instruction only—no discussion—no physical contact—no hints.

"There are steps going down. That was the last step. Turn to your left. Stretch out your arms."

I followed his instructions. It felt cold and the hair on my arms seemed to stand up like on a scared cat, but that could just be a nervous reaction to an unusual situation. Or it could be a static electric charge.

"Put down your arms. Turn right and walk forward. Stop. Turn left and stand still."

I stood there and waited for something to happen. Without thinking about it, both my hands arms rose, and I leaned forward. My open hands rested against a cold, solid surface.

He removed my blindfold, and said, "Open your eyes."

I saw then that my hands were on a wall. I was leaning against a wall that was covered with handprints. They weren't painted on, nor were they clearly defined. They were just smudgy marks but obviously from hundreds of slightly sweaty hands. I had just added mine to the collection. There was no doubt in my mind they were hand marks. It was eerily similar to the worn wall spots in North Battleford, except that in this case the material had not been worn away over a period of decades.

"Everyone I show this to does that," my friend said. "Do you want me to show you some other things?"

"No thanks, "I answered as calmly as I could. "Wilma is waiting in the car. I'd better go."

I got out of that place—fast.

I could expand on this story by telling you that my friend became insane (by every imaginable standard) some years later. The last time I saw him he said he was the 'Black Jesus', whatever he meant by that.

But I have no logical reason to conclude his mental instability was connected with the house in which he lived for two years. You might say his excessive drug use was the cause of his mental problems. Or was the drug use the result?

I just know I would never have lived there.

*

One evening Wilma and I went to a fancy Italian restaurant (replete with a gondola) for dinner. We were seated at a table for four with a large red napkin at each place. The waiter seated Wilma at one place and I sat opposite to her. I reached for my napkin and noticed, right in the center of my napkin, a small piece of something that looked like glass. It was shiny. I thought it might be a rhinestone so I picked it off the napkin and put it in my pocket.

A few days later, I examined the object and it seemed to be very shiny. Rather like a zircon. Wilma asked a jeweler and was told it was indeed a diamond worth $500. I phoned the restaurant on the chance it had fallen out of a ring belonging to one of their employees when they set the table.

When no one at the restaurant claimed it, I put a notice in the Winnipeg newspaper under lost and found (without naming the restaurant). When that didn't elicit any response, we put it in an envelope in our safety deposit box in the bank. Wilma printed the word, 'DIAMOND' in large letters on the envelope.

However, one time when I looked in the safety deposit box, the envelope with the diamond was gone. Wilma and I searched the contents of the box carefully, item by item, several times over a period of months. The diamond really was gone. This could obviously be explained away; it must have been left on the table when we took something out of the box, or had fallen on the floor.

If the story were to end here, it would just be a case of 'found and lost'.

Every time I opened the box after that I would leaf through all the papers just to see if maybe we had missed it somehow—still nothing.

And then, one day, about a year after the diamond had disappeared, I opened the box and there was the envelope, with the diamond in it, right on top of the pile of papers—in plain sight with the printing on top.

I have only three possible explanations (ignoring the diamond's initial sudden appearance):

1) Someone in the bank had taken it out of the safety deposit box, kept it for a year and then returned it. This is highly unlikely. Those boxes are supposed to be totally secure, and besides, if it had been taken for a year, why would the person return it?

2) Wilma had taken the diamond and later returned it as a joke on me. Knowing Wilma, and how disturbed she was about losing the diamond, this is even less likely.

3) Something supernatural was moving the diamond around as a message to me. If this were the case, then I totally missed the message.

I had the diamond set into a custom designed ring with a ruby on each side of the diamond (Ken and Anita's birthstone). The diamond still sits peacefully in Wilma's jewelry box. Maybe all it had wanted was to be loved or to be with other jewelry. Or maybe the setting is now too heavy for the spirit world to move it again.

*

My paternal grandmother was said to have the ability to foretell the future, although she denied it. She said she just knew things.

She said one time that Cliff's wife would have red hair, play the piano, and accompany Cliff when he played the violin. This wasn't a very elaborate prediction, but it did come true.

She was asked many times about my wife. Every time she said she couldn't see a wife or anything about me.

For many years, I was convinced I would never get married because of her comments. This was disturbing for me when I was in my twenties because one of my dreams was to live in a nice little house with a white picket fence and three children.

My grandmother had given me an additional piece of information, which I had ignored. She said that she had tried several times to have her fortune told, and had been rejected every time because, "I can't tell your fortune. You are yourself a fortuneteller, so it is impossible for anyone to tell yours." It seems this is some sort of a psychic rule.

Like my grandmother, I maintain I can't tell fortunes because I can't. However, every year or two I get a feeling about something that is so strong it scares me. I usually don't tell anyone because I don't think it would help to know the future. If you can't do anything to change it, how does it help to know it?

When our family was in California for Ken's July wedding, I was saying goodbye to Henry and Anita (who were living in Montreal) just as we were leaving to come home.

I started out to say to Henry, "I guess I won't be seeing you again until Christmas."

I had only got halfway through the sentence when I had a sudden realization that I would see him before Christmas, and it would be at a funeral. I broke off mid-sentence and walked away to recover. I assumed he would be dead the next time I saw him, and I didn't know what to do or say. I wanted to warn him or Anita, but all that would do was worry them.

I did see Henry 10 days later, but it was at his grandmother's funeral, not his.

*

There is a long stretch of highway between Winnipeg and Portage. It is smooth, straight, divided, free of trees that might hide deer wanting to cross, and has limited access. It was a sunny summer day without a single car in sight. My excuse was that I wanted to see how well my Triumph was running. I sped up to a bit over its cruising speed 100 mph (160 km/hr) and enjoyed the way it purred. When I got within a couple of miles of one of the few intersections, I eased off on the gas and let the car coast down to a more reasonable speed.

As I approached the intersection a police car pulled out in front of me and signaled for me to stop.

"Wait here until I get the reading of your speed."

This was in the early days of radar when the device was mounted on the side of the road using a little tripod. As I waited, and the police car pulled over the other cars as they came by, I wondered how far back the radar might have been. If it were more than a mile back I would be in serious trouble.

In court, the officer read his report, which included an assessment of my attitude when ticketed. He reported me as being 'cooperative'.

I almost laughed out loud. When he had told me I was clocked at 15 mph over the limit my attitude was more like 'ecstatic' or 'exuberant'. He was lucky I hadn't kissed him.

*

Gordon farmed the land around our garden. He was always friendly, happy, and loved to chat. No matter what he was doing he would stop to share a story or find something about which to talk. He was a good friend and always worked the land with loving care.

He was killed suddenly in a freak accident while working alone with machinery in the farmyard.

I bought a September Ruby apple tree that fall and planted it in his memory at the edge of our garden right next to a field where he had farmed. It was a young tree and I expected it would take two or three years to mature enough to bear fruit.

When spring came, I noticed the tree was healthy with a nice covering of leaves. The tree also had one, single white, blossom. This was surprising because apple blossoms invariably grow in clusters.

This single blossom set fruit, grew through the summer and by fall had produced a small, single, ruby red, apple, which grew to maturity and ripened.

It was as if Gordon's spirit was using this symbol as his way of saying his last words that he didn't have a chance to say to us.

***

Postscript

If you have traveled much (or had children grow up) you know that the human brain tends to forget unpleasant events and keep only the good memories. In writing this book, I have remembered some things that I had conveniently forgotten—like the time our flight to England was late causing us to miss a reservation in Amsterdam, or the night in Italy when I woke up with over a hundred bedbug bites and Wilma, sleeping next to me, got none.

Traveling overseas made me proud to be a Canadian. We always wore Canadian pins and received a friendly reception everywhere we went. At that time, the reputation of Canada was firmly established as being helpful in maintaining peace in countries that wanted help with their problems, rather than invading them and killing their people as some other countries seemed to do.

We may have been viewed as a bit boring, but harmless like an elderly uncle who mostly sat on the porch reading his Bible, but never told us what to do or preached at us. We used to think of politics as something necessary to maintain a civilized and pleasant life. There was a time (*many* years ago) when I didn't mind paying income taxes because I felt I was getting value for my money—I wasn't even concerned if I happened to pay a bit more than required. Politics was not considered to be some partisan chess game to be played and won at all costs, as seems to be happening more frequently lately.

Strangers have always been helpful to us, particularly overseas. Several times, when we needed directions and didn't speak the language, the person would motion for us to follow them and lead us to where we wanted to go, even though it might be a considerable distance out of their way.

When we lost our way, we even started saying, "We need to find a guide."

We always seemed to find one.

Writing this book has brought forth many good memories that have made me realize how much the people with whom I have interacted have meant to me. My seventy-five years have been a great trip with a cast of literally thousands if I include all the students I have met. I wish I could thank each of them personally. I realize I didn't thank them very much at the time when I was with them, but I guess that is just the way the world works.

Maybe I made it a more enjoyable for them to get where they were going, or at least made it a more interesting trip for them. I hope so.

Over the past years I have come to believe that everyone should be allowed to take an occasional mulligan* as they move through the golf-game of life. This is particularly true for young children and students in a classroom.

Older people shouldn't need a mulligan, because they have had lots of chances to make corrections. But it might still be nice to be given one now and then.

*Mulligan: A golf shot not counted against the score, after an unusually poor shot. It's like a "do-over."

COAT OF ARMS

S H I R R I F F

BLAZON OF ARMS

Arms: Azure on a fesse engrailed between three
griffin's heads erased or a fleur de lis of
the first between two roses gules.

Crest: A demi lion rampant or holding in the dexter
paw a branch of laurel argent berried gold.

Motto: Esse Quam Videri

"To be rather than to seem"

About the Author

Charles (Bill) Shirriff was born and raised in Saskatchewan during the Great Depression years of the 1930's. After graduation from the University of Manitoba with a Bachelor of Science in Mathematics, Physics and Chemistry, his love of learning and a penchant for new experiences led him to obtain a Master of Science in counseling psychology from the University of North Dakota and a B. A. degree from the State of New York. Over the years, he took additional courses in a variety of subjects at the University of Toronto, University of British Columbia, University of Connecticut (Storrs) and Stanford University in California.

His teaching career spanned 37 years. Thirty-five of them spent near Winnipeg, in the city of Portage la Prairie, where he held positions as teacher, counselor, Special Education Coordinator, and Consultant for the Gifted & Talented for the School Division.

Travel related to his vocation of teaching has taken him north to Swan River, Cranberry Portage, Flin Flon and Norway House.

A brief foray into the field of meteorology provided him with the opportunity to live in the tiny settlement of Moosonee, on the tip of James Bay, doing upper ozone atmosphere research for the International Geophysical Year in 1958.

In the early years of personal computers, Charles worked on the development of pressure sensitive keyboards for use by physically handicapped people. Charles operated a part-time small company to manufacture and sell the keyboards across Canada and in the United States for several years.

He has presented papers on computer-assisted learning provincially for Exceptional Children Conferences in Winnipeg; nationally at the National Research Council Symposium on Computer Technology in Vancouver; and internationally at the Association for the Development of Computer-Based Instructional Conference in Washington, D. C.

He has written two novels. The first, *Spirits of a Feather*, is based on the life of a gay teenager from an abusive and dysfunctional family and his struggle to make his way in the world.

The second novel, *Souls of a Feather*, is a sequel. It touches on Hutterian life, the Bahá'i faith, First Nations people, New Age philosophy, and other facets of our multicultural society.

Charles resides with his wife, Wilma, in Portage la Prairie, Manitoba, in their home overlooking beautiful Crescent Lake.

Their son, Ken, is a computer engineer with Google. He lives in California with his wife Kathryn and their daughter Sydney.

Their daughter, Anita, lives in Winnipeg with her husband, Henry, and their two daughters, Emma and Lillian.

Email: shirriff@gmail. com
Web site: shirriff.org

The Golden Rule

(the following examples are from various Internet sources and translated original sources)

Over thousands of years of human history, religions and philosophers in all parts of the world have tried to encapsulate a moral code of behavior into one simple saying. These attempts, although originally in a variety of languages, have produced strikingly similar messages.

This must mean something significant.

The fact that so many people seem to be unable to follow such a simple maxim is perhaps even more significant.

ARISTIPPUS OF CYRENE:
> -Cherish reciprocal benevolence, which will make you as anxious for another's welfare as your own.

BAHÀ'I:
> - Breathe not the sins of others so long as thou art thyself a sinner.
> - Choose thou for thy neighbor that which thou choosest for thyself.

BRAHMANISM:
> - Do naught unto others, which would cause you pain if done to you.

BUDDHIST:
> - Hurt not others with that which pains you.

CHRISTIANITY:
> - And as ye would that men should do to you, do ye also to them likewise.

CONFUCIAN:
> - Try your best to treat others, as you would wish to be treated yourself.

EGYPTIAN (ANCIENT):

- Do for one who may do for you, that you may cause him thus to do.

FIRST NATION (North American Indian):

- Grant that I may not judge my neighbor until I have walked a mile in his moccasins.
- Respect for all life is the foundation.

GREEK:

- Do not do to others what you would not wish to suffer yourself (Isocrates).
- May I do to others as I would that they should do unto me (Plato).

HINDU:

- This is the sum of duty: do naught to others, which if done to thee would cause thee pain.

HUMANISM:

- Don't do things you wouldn't want to have done to you.

HUTTERIAN BRETHREN:

- What's mine is yours. What's yours is mine.

ISLAMIC:

- Not one of you is a believer until he loves for his brother what he loves for himself.
- Not do to others that which would anger you if others did it to you.

JAINISM:

- A man should wander about treating all creatures as he himself would be treated.

JUDAISM:

- What is hateful to you; do not to your fellow man. That is the law: all the rest is commentary.

NIGERIAN SAYING (Yoruba):

- One going to take a pointed stick to pinch a baby bird should first try it on himself to feel how it hurts.

ROMAN PAGAN RELIGION:
- The law imprinted on the hearts of all men is to love the members of society as themselves.

SCIENTOLOGY:
- Try to treat others as you would want them to treat you.

SENECA:
- Treat your inferiors as you would be treated by your superiors.

SEXTUS (a Pythagorean):
- What you wish your neighbors to be to you, such be also to them.

SHINTO:
- The heart of the person before you is a mirror. See there your own form.

SIKHISM:
- Don't create enmity with anyone, as God is within everyone.

SOCRATES:
- Do not do to others that which would anger you if others did it to you.

SUFISM:
- If you haven't the will to gladden someone's heart, then at least beware lest you hurt someone's heart.

TAOIST:
- Regard your neighbor's gain as your own gain, and your neighbor's loss as your own loss.

THALES:
- Avoid doing what you would blame others for doing.

UNITARIAN:
- Justice, equity and compassion in human relations . . .

WICCA:
- As in it harm no one, do what thou wilt.
- Do whatever you want, as long as it harms no one including yourself.

ZOROASTRIAN:
- Whatever is disagreeable to you, do not do unto others.

***

STANDARD MODERN:
    - Do unto others, as you would have them do unto you.

PARANOID MODERN:
    - Do unto others before they do unto you.

CYNICAL MODERN:
    - He who has the Gold, makes the Rule.

MODERN POLITICAL:
    - He who makes the rules, gets to break them.